one
sheet
eats

one sheet eats

100+ DELICIOUS RECIPES ALL MADE ON A BAKING SHEET

©2017 Time Inc. Books

Published by Oxmoor House, an imprint of Time Inc.
Books 225 Liberty Street, New York, NY 10281

Assistant Editor: April Smitherman Colburn
Project Editors: Melissa Brown, Lacie Pinyan
Design Director: Melissa Clark
Photo Director: Paden Reich
Designer: Allison Chi
Photographers: Antonis Achilleos, Daniel Agee,
    Annabelle Breakey, Jennifer Causey,
    Jennifer Davick, Stephen DeVries, Beth Dreiling
    Hontzas, John Kernick, Becky Luigart-Stayner,
    Randy Mayor, Oxmoor House Staff, Brie Passano,
    Kate Sears, Time Inc. Food Studios
Prop Stylists: Ginny Branch, Missie Neville Crawford
    Thom Driver, Time Inc. Food Studios
Food Stylists: Katelyn Hardwick, Tina Stamos,
    Time Inc Food Studios
Prop Coordinator: Audrey Davis
Recipe Developers and Testers: David Bonom,
    Cooking Light Test Kitchen, Dana Cowin,
    Emma Crist, Paige Grandjean, Aglaia Kremezi,
    Sally Kuzemchak, April McGreger, Oxmoor House
    Test Kitchen, Sara Quessenberry, Southern Living
    Test Kitchen, Sunset Test Kitchen, Time Inc. Food
    Studios, Virginia Willis
Senior Production Manager: Greg A. Amason

Assistant Production and Project Manager:
    Lauren Moriarty
Copy Editors: Adrienne Davis, Jacqueline Giovanelli
Indexer: Mary Ann Laurens
Fellows: Helena Joseph, Kaitlyn Pacheco,
    Hanna Yokeley

ISBN-13: 978-0-8487-5449-5
Library of Congress Control Number: 2017942366

First Edition 2017
Printed in the United States of America
10 9 8 7 6 5 4 3 2 1

We welcome your comments and suggestions about
Time Inc. Books.

Time Inc. Books
Attention: Book Editors
P.O. Box 62310
Tampa, Florida 33662-2310

Time Inc. Books products may be purchased for
business or promotional use. For information on bulk
purchases, please contact Christi Crowley in the
Special Sales Department at (845) 895-9858.

contents

baking sheet cheat sheet

Quick Facts to Know About the Handiest Pan You Own

A NOTE ABOUT THIS COOKBOOK

The recipes contained in these pages are dedicated to simplifying home cooking. (Who doesn't want to make meal prep easier?) Each recipe requires only one type of bakeware or cookware: a baking sheet. Forget all other pots, pans, and baking dishes! By using a baking sheet (sometimes two) and a few prep items found in most kitchens, such as mixing bowls, a food processor, a blender, a microwave, and a wire rack, anyone can make delicious foods from a complete dinner (check out the one-sheet meals found in Main Dishes) to simple side dishes, crowd-pleasing appetizers, and more. With these recipes crafted for simple, clutter-free, and satisfying cooking, making food will be a joyous event in your kitchen.

Is that a baking sheet?

With many different types of pans in today's kitchens, it's necessary to define exactly what a baking sheet is and how it differs from other items used for cooking and baking. For starters, the terms sheet pan, baking tray, and rimmed baking sheet are synonymous with the term baking sheet. The difference between these items and other vessels lies in their shape. Baking sheets are flat rectangular sheets of metal (sometimes ceramic) with four rolled edges, about 1-inch deep, that are used to bake foods inside an oven. Though baking sheets all have this same structure, they come in a variety of lengths and widths, and even different manufacturers may produce slightly different sizes. However, there are dimensions that are generally considered to be standard. See page 8 for a chart of these common sizes.

Sometimes people refer to all baking sheets as jelly-roll pans, but they are not always correct to do so. A jelly-roll pan is a specific size of baking sheet, one that is roughly 15½- x 10½- x 1-inches. So, while all jelly-roll pans are baking sheets, baking sheets are not all jelly-roll pans. Similarly, many people incorrectly use the term baking sheet interchangeably with cookie sheet—and understandably so, for cookies can indeed be made on a baking sheet. However, there is one distinguishing difference between the two: A cookie sheet does not have the rolled edges that a baking sheet has; instead, cookie sheets are rimless. This is so that the delicate cookies can slide off the sheet's surface. Some cookie sheets have one side or two parallel sides that are slightly raised. These lips serve as a handle, making it easier to grab the hot sheet from the oven.

Moreover, another important distinction to make is the difference between baking sheets and baking pans. Baking pans are deeper and come in a variety of shapes. The most common type of baking pan is the standard 13- x 9-inch pan with sides that are 2 inches deep. Baking pans also come in square sizes, normally 8- x 8-inch or 9- x 9-inch. Other common varieties of baking pans are cake pans, fluted cake pans, muffin pans, loaf pans, and pie pans. Traditionally, if the pan is made of metal it is called a baking pan, and those items made of glass, ceramic, or other heat-proof materials are called baking dishes.

Every recipe here assumes that the baking sheet used will have four rimmed edges of about 1-inch depth. Unless a size is given, a half-sized baking sheet will work well, and even if a smaller sheet is called for, say a jelly-roll pan, using a larger sheet, if that's all you have on hand, will suffice. Do realize that full-size baking sheets are mainly for commercial use and won't fit in most home ovens.

Ovenware 101

With all the varying terminology used when talking about various cooking and baking tools, it's easy to get confused. Here's a simple guide to the standard sheets, pans, and dishes.

Flat or 1-inch Deep

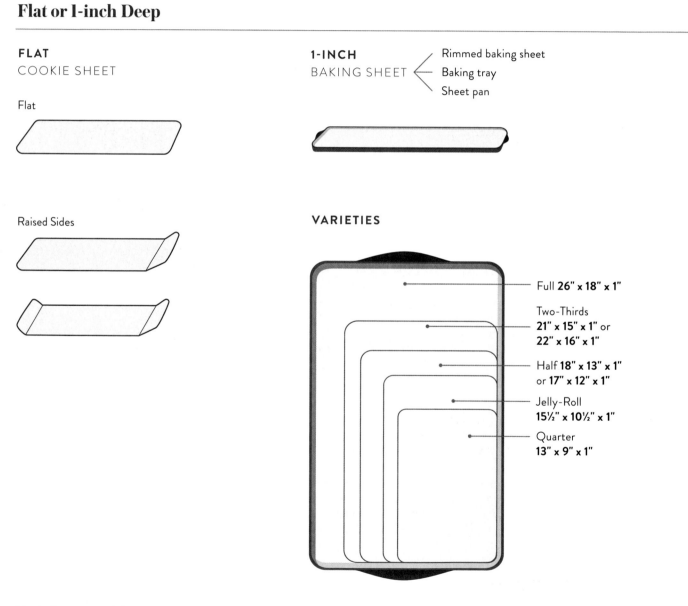

FLAT
COOKIE SHEET

Flat

Raised Sides

1-INCH
BAKING SHEET ← Rimmed baking sheet
Baking tray
Sheet pan

VARIETIES

Full **26" x 18" x 1"**

Two-Thirds
21" x 15" x 1" or
22" x 16" x 1"

Half **18" x 13" x 1"**
or **17" x 12" x 1"**

Jelly-Roll
15½" x 10½" x 1"

Quarter
13" x 9" x 1"

(Again, keep in mind that dimensions may vary slightly depending on the manufacturer.)

one sheet eats

More Than 1-inch Deep

BAKING PAN
METAL

BAKING DISH
GLASS, CERAMIC, ETC.

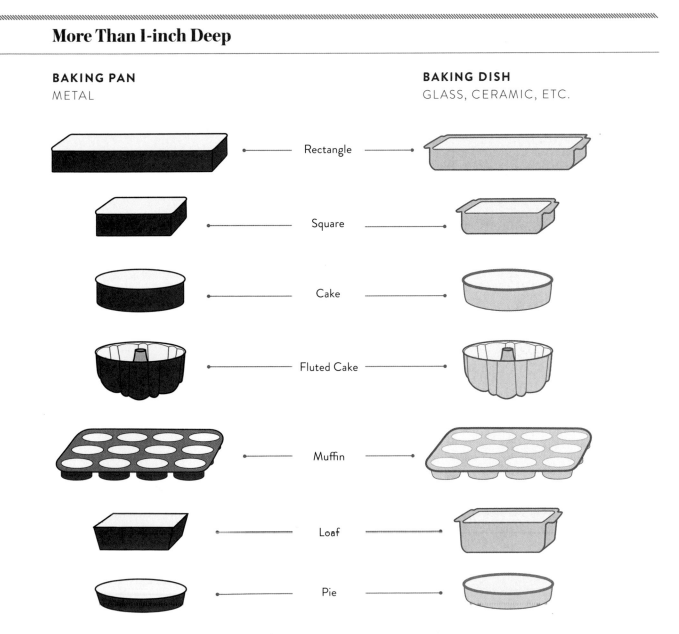

Rectangle

Square

Cake

Fluted Cake

Muffin

Loaf

Pie

How does it work?

A baking sheet's sides are key to its magic. They lock in juices, or even dough, that otherwise would drip over the sheet into the oven. Trapping the moisture keeps the oven clean and keeps foods from drying out. Any dish made on a cookie sheet can be made on a baking sheet, but the reverse statement is not true. This makes a baking sheet the more versatile of the two and, therefore, a must-have item for home cooks wanting to minimize the number of kitchen tools they use.

Should I use a light or dark sheet?

Because dark metal sheets conduct heat better than their lighter counterparts, they will brown cookies, biscuits, and other baked goods faster. To cook foods more slowly and evenly and with less browning, use a lighter metal sheet. Ceramic baking sheets function similarly to light metal sheets. If a recipe specifically calls for a light sheet and you only have a dark one, it's fine; just slightly reduce the heat and perhaps reduce the bake time, too. If the recipe doesn't specify which type to use, you're okay to use whichever you have.

How can I make it last?

Properly maintaining your baking sheet can allow you to use it for years. The first rule of maintenance is to let your hot baking sheet cool completely before rinsing it. After removing the cooked food from it, you might be tempted to run water over it to keep any residual foods from sticking—don't! Cooling the sheet too fast can cause warping, and when the bottom of the pan isn't even, it won't be able to evenly brown foods. If food becomes stuck to the sheet while cooling (or during the baking process) and isn't easily removed when the cooled sheet is lightly scrubbed under warm water, the best thing to do is fill the sheet with warm, soapy water and let it soak for at least 30 minutes before scrubbing again. Don't use steel wool or other harsh abrasives on a new or nonstick baking sheet, as they will scratch its surface. It's generally a good idea to hand wash your baking sheet. Putting nonstick products in the dishwasher can remove their coating, and all aluminum can be discolored in the dishwasher. Ceramic pans, which are nonstick, can sometimes be the exception. In any case, be sure to check the manufacturer's instructions before putting any baking sheet in the dishwasher.

Over time, your baking sheet will develop dark spots, areas of the sheet that char during baking due to uneven heat distribution (often due to a warped sheet) or overcooking food. Though sheets with dark spots can still be used to great effect, it's also true that dark spots can alter your cooking results. Dark spots conduct heat more quickly than the surrounding uncharred areas and can lead to uneven cooking. With a quick Internet search, you'll find many commercial products available, as well as handy home solutions, to remove dark spots. Furthermore, lining your baking sheet with parchment paper or aluminum foil is a great way to keep it clean.

Should I use parchment paper or aluminum foil?

The primary reason for lining your baking sheet with parchment paper or foil is to make sure foods don't stick and to make cleanup a cinch. The two liners can often be used interchangeably, but be sure to use parchment paper, which is nonstick, for dough and any food that might cling to the lining. If you have only aluminum foil on hand, coat it with cooking spray to make it nonstick.

A NOTE ABOUT NONSTICK SHEETS
They're perfectly fine to use, but like all nonstick material the coating will wear off and you'll be left needing to purchase a new one.

appetizers & snacks

These slightly sweet bite-sized tartlets made with flaky puff pastry are the perfect crowd-pleasing snack. Use orange, red, and yellow baby bell peppers for the prettiest presentation.

tomato–baby bell pepper tartlets

SERVES **10**   HANDS-ON TIME: **30 MINUTES**   TOTAL TIME: **55 MINUTES**

1 sheet frozen puff pastry dough, thawed
1 ounce Parmigiano-Reggiano cheese, grated (about ¼ cup)
2 tablespoons canola mayonnaise
1 small garlic clove, minced
8 grape tomatoes, cut into ⅛-inch-thick slices
3 baby bell peppers, cut into ⅛-inch-thick rings
2 teaspoons fresh thyme leaves

1 Preheat the oven to 400°F.

2 Line a baking sheet with parchment paper.

3 Unfold the dough; place on a work surface lightly dusted with flour. Roll gently into a 10- x 9-inch rectangle. Cut the dough into 20 (2¼- x 2-inch) rectangles. Score each rectangle about ⅛-inch from the edge. Prick each dough piece liberally with a fork. Arrange the dough pieces on the prepared baking sheet; chill 10 minutes.

4 Combine the cheese, mayonnaise, and garlic, stirring well. Spread a scant ½ teaspoon of the cheese mixture over each dough piece. Top each tartlet with about 2 tomato slices and 2 bell pepper rings. Bake at 400°F until the dough is lightly browned, about 15 minutes. Remove from the oven, and sprinkle evenly with the thyme.

If you or your guests are not beet fans, substitute sweet potatoes: Clean 4 (4-ounce) sweet potatoes and pierce each 5 to 6 times with a fork. Place the potatoes directly on a microwave-safe plate and microwave at HIGH 8 to 10 minutes, or until fork tender, turning once halfway through. Then cool, peel, and slice.

tricolored beet tart

SERVES **12**   HANDS-ON TIME: **24 MINUTES**   TOTAL TIME: **1 HOUR, 50 MINUTES**

5 small red, gold, and Chioggia beets
   (about 1½ pounds)
1 tablespoon water
1 sheet frozen puff pastry dough, thawed
1 tablespoon fresh orange juice
1½ teaspoons honey
1½ tablespoons chopped hazelnuts, toasted
1½ teaspoons fresh thyme leaves
½ teaspoon flaked sea salt (such as Maldon)
1½ ounces goat cheese, crumbled (about ⅓ cup)

1 Preheat the oven to 400°F.

2 Place the beets on a large piece of aluminum foil; bring the edges of the foil to the center. Add the water to the beets; crimp the edges of the foil to seal. Bake at 400°F until the beets are tender when pierced with a fork, about 1 hour. Remove the foil; discard. When cool enough to handle, peel the beets, and thinly slice using a mandoline or sharp knife.

3 Roll out the puff pastry sheet to a 14- x 12-inch rectangle on a large piece of parchment paper. Place the parchment paper with the puff pastry on a baking sheet. Score a 1-inch border around the edge of the puff pastry with a paring knife; prick the area inside the border several times with a fork. Bake the pastry at 400°F until light golden, about 14 minutes; remove from the oven.

4 Arrange the beet slices over the puff pastry, inside the border, so that the slices overlap by about ½ inch. Bake at 400°F until the crust is golden brown, about 12 minutes. Brush the orange juice over the beets; drizzle with the honey. Sprinkle the hazelnuts, thyme, salt, and goat cheese over the tart. Cut into 12 slices.

flavor note

Slightly sweeter than other beets, Chioggia beets are an Italian heirloom variety marked by their concentric red and white interior rings. Baking the beets will muddy the contrast of the ring colors.

Unlike classic pesto, this filling contains no oil. Once everything is minced in the food processor, though, it develops a paste-like consistency. Thaw the pastry in the fridge overnight, or leave out at room temperature for an hour or two. (Also pictured on page 12)

pesto pastries

SERVES **10**   HANDS-ON TIME: **20 MINUTES**   TOTAL TIME: **46 MINUTES**

2 tablespoons pine nuts, toasted
1 garlic clove, chopped
3 tablespoons grated Parmigiano-Reggiano cheese
2 (1-ounce) packages fresh basil, plus more for garnish (optional)
1 sheet frozen puff pastry dough, thawed
⅜ teaspoon kosher salt

1 Preheat the oven to 400°F.

2 Line a baking sheet with parchment paper.

3 Place the nuts and garlic in a mini food processor; pulse until finely chopped. Add the cheese; pulse to combine. Remove the large stems from the basil. Tear the leaves, and add to the processor; process until very finely chopped and almost paste-like.

4 Unfold the dough; place on a work surface lightly dusted with flour. Roll gently into a 10- x 9-inch rectangle. Spread the pesto over the dough all the way to the edges. Sprinkle with the salt. Roll up both long sides of the dough, jelly-roll fashion, until they meet in the middle. Place in the freezer for 10 minutes.

5 Cut the dough roll crosswise into 20 slices. Arrange the slices in a single layer on the prepared baking sheet. Bake at 400°F until lightly browned, about 16 minutes. Garnish with additional basil leaves, if desired.

Serve these golden rolls at your next patio party or Mediterranean-inspired dinner gathering. Freeze leftover rolls up to 6 months. To reheat, cover loosely with foil and bake at 375°F for 15 minutes. Uncover and bake 10 minutes, turning after 5 minutes.

spinach, herb, AND cheese phyllo rolls

SERVES **15**   HANDS-ON TIME: **50 MINUTES**   TOTAL TIME: **2 HOURS**

¾ cup chopped fresh flat-leaf parsley
½ cup finely chopped shallots
½ cup finely chopped green onions
½ cup finely chopped fresh dill
¼ cup chopped fresh mint leaves
1½ tablespoons chopped fresh thyme
12 ounces baby spinach leaves, coarsely chopped
6 tablespoons extra-virgin olive oil
¼ teaspoon freshly ground black pepper
1 large egg, lightly beaten
3 ounces feta cheese, crumbled (about ¾ cup)
20 (14- x 9-inch) frozen phyllo sheets, thawed
   (about 8 ounces)

1 Preheat the oven to 375°F.

2 Combine the parsley, shallots, green onions, dill, mint, thyme, and spinach in a large bowl. Add 3 tablespoons of the oil; stir well to combine. Stir in the pepper, egg, and cheese until well blended.

3 Line a baking sheet with parchment paper; coat well with cooking spray.

4 Working with 2 phyllo sheets at a time (cover the remaining dough to prevent drying), brush 2 sheets lightly with the remaining olive oil (the long edge of the sheets should be closest to you). Top with 2 phyllo sheets; brush lightly with the oil. Arrange 2 cups of the spinach mixture in an even mound along the phyllo edge nearest you, leaving a 1-inch border on either side. Fold the sides of the phyllo partially over the mound; roll the dough and filling, burrito-style, to form an 11- x 3-inch roll. Place the roll, seam side down, on the prepared pan. Repeat the procedure with the remaining dough, oil, and filling to form 5 rolls. Make 3 small slits in the top of each roll to allow the steam to escape.

5 Bake the rolls at 375°F until golden brown and crisp, about 50 minutes. Carefully transfer to a wire rack; cool 20 minutes. Cut each roll diagonally into 6 slices.

When prep time is short, these quick and easy-to-make shells are the perfect go-to appetizer. Filled with traditional spanakopita ingredients—spinach, feta cheese, and egg—they're a simplified version of sister spanakopita recipes (like the one on page 20) yet offer the same great flavor.

spanakopita bites

SERVES **15**   HANDS-ON TIME: **7 MINUTES**   TOTAL TIME: **17 MINUTES**

2 (1.9-ounce) packages mini phyllo shells
   (such as Athens)
1 (10-ounce) package frozen chopped spinach,
   thawed, drained, and squeezed dry
1 (4-ounce) package crumbled feta cheese with
   lemon, garlic, and oregano
2 large eggs, beaten
½ teaspoon freshly ground black pepper, plus more
   for garnish (optional)
Kosher salt (optional)

1 Preheat the oven to 375°F.

2 Place the phyllo shells on a large baking sheet. Combine the spinach and remaining ingredients in a medium bowl. Spoon the filling evenly into the shells.

3 Bake at 375°F until the filling is set (the shells will be lightly browned), about 10 minutes. Garnish with salt and additional pepper, if desired.

flavor note

A sprinkling of chopped fresh dill before serving adds an additional dose of Mediterranean flavor.

Making bruschetta is a smart way to use bread that's beginning to pass its prime. Here, the baguette is toasted, and then topped with bursting, roasted cherry tomatoes and creamy ricotta mixed with a host of Italian herbs. (Also pictured on page 12)

lemony herbed ricotta AND roasted tomato bruschetta

SERVES **8**　HANDS-ON TIME: **5 MINUTES**　TOTAL TIME: **28 MINUTES**

1 (4-ounce) whole-wheat French bread baguette
1 pint cherry tomatoes
1 tablespoon olive oil
⅜ teaspoon kosher salt
⅜ teaspoon freshly ground black pepper
¼ teaspoon sugar
2 tablespoons chopped fresh basil
1 tablespoon fresh thyme leaves
1 tablespoon chopped fresh oregano
1 teaspoon grated lemon rind
1 tablespoon fresh lemon juice
6 ounces ricotta cheese (about ¾ cup)

1 Preheat the broiler.

2 Coat a baking sheet with cooking spray.

3 Slice the baguette into 8 thin slices; arrange on the baking sheet. Toast the bread under the broiler until golden brown, about 3 minutes, turning the slices halfway through. Remove from the oven. Remove the bread from the baking sheet.

4 Reduce the oven temperature to 450°F. Toss the cherry tomatoes with the oil, ¼ teaspoon each of the salt and pepper, and sugar; place the tomatoes on the baking sheet and bake at 450°F for 20 minutes. Using a rubber spatula, fold the basil, thyme leaves, oregano, lemon rind, and lemon juice into the ricotta. Spread 1½ tablespoons of the ricotta mixture evenly over each toast; top with the roasted tomatoes. Sprinkle the toasts evenly with the remaining ⅛ teaspoon each of salt and pepper.

Chicken and waffles can be an indulgent dinner. Impress guests by serving them this quick-and-easy appetizer version that uses chicken tenders and a buttermilk batter as a fun before-dinner treat. If desired, serve with dill pickle slices, which will give a tangy brightness to the dish.

chicken AND mini waffles WITH spiced honey

SERVES **24**   HANDS-ON TIME: **10 MINUTES**   TOTAL TIME: **1 HOUR, 6 MINUTES**

12 chicken breast tenders, each cut in half crosswise (1 pound, 10 ounces)
¾ cup buttermilk
1½ cups panko (Japanese breadcrumbs)
½ teaspoon garlic powder
¼ teaspoon smoked paprika
¼ teaspoon freshly ground black pepper
¼ teaspoon table salt
Cooking spray
24 whole-grain mini waffles
¾ cup honey
¾ teaspoon ground cinnamon
½ teaspoon grated peeled fresh ginger
½ teaspoon hot sauce

1 Stir together the chicken and buttermilk in a medium bowl. Chill 30 minutes. Place a large baking sheet in the oven, and preheat the oven to 450°F.

2 Place the panko in a shallow bowl. Stir together the garlic powder and next 3 ingredients. Remove the chicken from the buttermilk, and pat dry; discard the buttermilk.

3 Sprinkle the chicken evenly with the spice mixture; dredge in the panko. Remove the baking sheet from the oven; coat with the cooking spray. Immediately place the chicken on the hot baking sheet; coat the chicken with the cooking spray.

4 Bake at 450°F until the chicken is crisp and lightly browned, about 20 to 25 minutes.

5 Arrange the waffles on a wire rack on a jelly-roll pan. Bake at 450°F until toasted, about 3 minutes on each side.

6 Meanwhile, stir together the honey and the remaining 3 ingredients in a small microwave-safe bowl. Microwave at HIGH 30 seconds or until warm.

7 Place the waffles on a serving platter; top the waffles with the chicken, and drizzle with the honey mixture. Serve immediately.

This spicy two-bite appetizer is perfect for an at-home game-day viewing party. Use leftover cooked chicken breasts or finely chop store-bought rotisserie chicken.

party poppers

SERVES **6**   HANDS-ON TIME: **20 MINUTES**   TOTAL TIME: **52 MINUTES**

12 medium jalapeño chiles
1 (8-ounce) package cream cheese, softened
1 cup finely chopped cooked chicken
2 tablespoons finely chopped fresh cilantro
1 tablespoon fresh lime juice
¾ teaspoon kosher salt
12 hickory-smoked bacon slices, cut in half
24 wooden picks

1 Preheat the oven to 400°F.

2 Line a baking sheet with aluminum foil. Spray a wire rack with cooking spray.

3 Cut each chile in half lengthwise; remove the seeds and membranes.

4 Stir together the cream cheese, chicken, cilantro, lime juice, and salt. Spoon 1½ to 2 teaspoons of the chicken mixture into each chile half, spreading to fill the cavity. Wrap each half with a bacon piece, and secure with a wooden pick. Place the poppers on the prepared wire rack on the baking sheet.

5 Bake at 400°F until the bacon begins to crisp and the chiles are softened, about 25 minutes. Increase the oven temperature to broil, and broil until the bacon is crisp, 2 to 3 minutes. Let stand 5 minutes before serving.

prep pointer

Yes, you can cook bacon in your oven (and this trick is especially handy when you want to cook bacon for a crowd)! Simply place a wire rack on a baking sheet, line the rack with uncooked bacon strips, and bake at 375°F for about 15 minutes. Turn the bacon over halfway through for the crispiest results. Lining the pan with aluminum foil will make cleanup easier.

Requiring just three ingredients plus your favorite dipping condiment—we call for Dijon mustard here—these tasty bites couldn't be simpler to make. You can substitute Cheddar cheese for the pepper Jack, depending on what you have on hand.

southwestern pigs IN A blanket

SERVES **8 TO 10**   HANDS-ON TIME: **5 MINUTES**   TOTAL TIME: **17 MINUTES**

2 (8-ounce) cans refrigerated crescent rolls
1 (8-ounce) package presliced pepper Jack cheese
2 (9.6-ounce) packages fully cooked breakfast
  sausage links (such as Jimmy Dean)
Dijon mustard

1 Preheat the oven to 375°F.

2 Line a baking sheet with parchment paper.

3 Divide the crescent rolls into individual triangles. Cut each of 4 pepper Jack slices into 4 pieces. Place 1 pepper Jack piece and 1 fully cooked breakfast sausage link in the center of each dough triangle. Roll up, starting at the wide end. Arrange on the prepared baking sheet.

4 Bake at 375°F until golden brown, about 12 minutes. Serve with the Dijon mustard.

Heat up the party with these peppery Mexican-style chorizo sausage balls. A pinch of cinnamon and a few scoops of plum jelly give this savory nibble a slightly sweet, complex flavor.

sweet potato AND chorizo sausage bites

SERVES **12**   HANDS-ON TIME: **20 MINUTES**   TOTAL TIME: **40 MINUTES**

1 pound fresh Mexican chorizo sausage, casings removed

2¼ cups all-purpose baking mix (such as Bisquick)

1 (8-ounce) package pre-shredded extra-sharp Cheddar cheese

½ cup chilled mashed roasted sweet potato (from 1 sweet potato)

⅛ teaspoon ground cinnamon

⅛ teaspoon kosher salt

6 tablespoons plum jam or scuppernong jelly

2 tablespoons Dijon mustard

1 Preheat the oven to 350°F.

2 Lightly coat a baking sheet with cooking spray.

3 Stir together the sausage, baking mix, Cheddar, mashed sweet potato, cinnamon, and salt in a large bowl. Roll into 48 (1½-inch) balls, and place about 1 inch apart on the prepared baking sheet. Bake at 350°F until the sausage balls are cooked through and golden brown, about 20 minutes.

4 Stir together the jelly and mustard in a small bowl until well blended. (If your jelly is too stiff to blend, microwave the mixture at HIGH in 15-second increments until soft enough to stir.) Serve with the sausage balls.

prep pointer

To get the ½ cup of mashed sweet potato needed here, microwave 1 medium fork-pierced sweet potato at HIGH 5 to 6 minutes, turning once halfway through. Then cool, peel, slice, and mash.

If you've ever struggled with the "What should I bring?" dilemma when heading to a potluck, look no further than this delicious and easily portable dish. Make the potatoes the day before your get-together, and refrigerate until you leave. When you arrive, they'll be the right serving temperature. (Also pictured on page 13)

deviled potatoes

SERVES **10**   HANDS-ON TIME: **25 MINUTES**   TOTAL TIME: **2 HOURS**

1 pound baby red potatoes (about 15)

1 tablespoon olive oil

1½ teaspoons kosher salt

½ cup sour cream

2 tablespoons brined capers, drained and rinsed

2 teaspoons chopped fresh flat-leaf parsley, plus more for garnish (optional)

2 teaspoons chopped fresh dill, plus more for garnish (optional)

2 teaspoons whole-grain mustard

1 teaspoon lemon rind, plus more for garnish (optional)

1 Preheat the oven to 350°F.

2 Place the potatoes in a small bowl, and drizzle with the oil. Sprinkle with 1 teaspoon of the salt; toss to coat. Spread the potatoes in a single layer on a baking sheet, and bake at 350°F until tender when pierced, about 40 minutes. Remove from the oven; cool 15 minutes.

3 Cut each potato in half crosswise. Carefully scoop out the potato pulp into a medium bowl, leaving the shells intact. Place the shells, cut sides up, on the baking sheet, and bake at 350°F until dry, about 10 more minutes. Cool completely, about 30 minutes.

4 Stir together the potato pulp, sour cream, capers, parsley, dill, mustard, rind, and the remaining ½ teaspoon salt. Spoon the mixture generously into each potato shell. Garnish with additional chopped fresh flat-leaf parsley, fresh dill, and lemon rind, if desired.

This chip and dip combo is full of flavor and is a cinch to make. Bake the pita wedges until they're crisp, and then blend together roasted red bell peppers with almonds and other high-flavor ingredients. It makes a great after-school snack for kids or happy-hour accompaniment for your favorite cocktail.

homemade pita chips WITH red pepper dip

SERVES **8**   HANDS-ON TIME: **10 MINUTES**   TOTAL TIME: **16 MINUTES**

Cooking spray
2 (6-inch) whole-wheat pitas
¼ teaspoon kosher salt
¼ teaspoon paprika
1 cup bottled roasted red bell peppers
¼ cup Marcona almonds or dry-roasted almonds (about 1¼ ounces)
1 tablespoon extra-virgin olive oil
1½ teaspoons red wine vinegar
1 teaspoon minced fresh garlic
½ teaspoon ground cumin
⅛ teaspoon ground red pepper
⅛ teaspoon freshly ground black pepper
1 teaspoon chopped fresh chives (optional)

1 Preheat the oven to 400°F.

2 Coat a baking sheet with cooking spray.

3 Cut each pita into 16 wedges. Carefully peel apart each wedge to make 2 thinner wedges. Arrange the wedges in a single layer on the prepared baking sheet. Lightly coat the wedges with the cooking spray; sprinkle with ⅛ teaspoon each of the salt and paprika. Bake at 400°F until lightly browned and crisp, about 6 minutes.

4 While the chips bake, place the bell peppers, almonds, oil, red wine vinegar, garlic, cumin, red pepper, and black pepper in a blender; add the remaining ⅛ teaspoon each salt and paprika. Blend until smooth; garnish with the chives, if desired. Serve with the chips.

Sugar- and cinnamon–dusted tortilla chips make the perfect pairing for this sweet and spicy salsa. Make the chips in advance, cool completely, and store in an airtight container until ready to serve.

strawberry-avocado salsa WITH cinnamon tortilla chips

SERVES **12**   HANDS-ON TIME: **10 MINUTES**   TOTAL TIME: **20 MINUTES**

2 teaspoons canola oil

6 (6-inch) whole-wheat flour tortillas

2 teaspoons sugar

½ teaspoon ground cinnamon

1½ cups finely chopped ripe avocado (about 2)

1 cup finely chopped fresh strawberries

2 tablespoons minced fresh cilantro

1 teaspoon minced seeded jalapeño chile

2 teaspoons fresh lime juice

⅜ teaspoon table salt

1 Preheat the oven to 350°F.

2 Brush the oil evenly over one side of each tortilla. Combine the sugar and cinnamon; sprinkle evenly over the oil-coated sides of the tortillas. Cut each tortilla into 12 wedges; arrange the wedges in a single layer on two baking sheets. Bake at 350°F until crisp, about 10 minutes.

3 Combine the avocado and the remaining ingredients; stir gently to combine. Serve with the chips.

prep pointer

An avocado is ripe when it gives slightly but is not mushy when firmly grasped. You can also determine ripeness by checking under the avocado's small stem. If the color beneath is green, it is ripe; if the color is brown, it's overripe.

Spice up traditional snack mix with Asian ingredients like wasabi peas, toasted sesame oil, soy sauce, cashews, and ground ginger. Once the mix cools, serve it to party guests directly from the baking sheet, or scoop it into zip-top plastic bags and include in kids' lunch boxes, a briefcase, or a purse for a midday snack.

sesame-soy-nut AND **pretzel snack mix**

SERVES **8**   HANDS-ON TIME: **5 MINUTES**   TOTAL TIME: **35 MINUTES**

1 cup unsalted miniature pretzels
1 cup whole-wheat cereal squares (such as Chex)
¾ cup wasabi peas
⅔ cup unsalted roasted cashew halves
2 tablespoons canola oil
1 tablespoon toasted sesame oil
1 tablespoon soy sauce
1 teaspoon garlic powder
1 teaspoon ground ginger
¼ teaspoon ground red pepper
4 cups unsalted air-popped popcorn

1 Preheat the oven to 250°F.

2 Combine the pretzels, cereal squares, wasabi peas, and cashew halves in a large bowl. Combine the canola oil, sesame oil, soy sauce, garlic powder, ground ginger, and ground red pepper, stirring with a whisk. Drizzle the oil mixture over the pretzel mixture; toss to coat. Add the popcorn; toss.

3 Spread the popcorn mixture in a single layer on a baking sheet. Bake at 250°F for 30 minutes, stirring once after 15 minutes. Cool completely. Store the snack mix in an airtight container up to 1 week.

Make a double batch and divide it in two. Serve with yogurt, and you have a supereasy breakfast for Saturday. Store the other batch in an airtight container for a quick Monday-morning breakfast.

orange, pumpkin seed, AND smoked almond granola

SERVES **4**   HANDS-ON TIME: **5 MINUTES**   TOTAL TIME: **31 MINUTES**

½ cup old-fashioned rolled oats
¼ cup roasted unsalted pumpkin seeds
1 ounce lightly salted smoked almonds, chopped
5 teaspoons brown sugar
1½ tablespoons canola oil
1 teaspoon grated orange rind
1 tablespoon fresh orange juice
¼ teaspoon vanilla extract
⅛ teaspoon table salt

1 Preheat the oven to 325°F.

2 Line a baking sheet with parchment paper.

3 Combine all the ingredients in a medium bowl, stirring well with a spatula. Spread the mixture on the prepared baking sheet. Bake at 325°F for 26 minutes. Cool completely. Store the granola in an airtight container up to 1 week.

flavor note

For a subtle bit of added chewy texture and sweetness, add ¼ cup large unsweetened coconut flakes to the mixture before baking.

Use these nuts in both sweet and savory dishes. Top a tart for a cinnamony sweet and crunchy finish, or crack them and sprinkle over chicken salad. They're good on their own, too! You can change the flavor to suit many tastes: In place of cinnamon, try a little garam masala for an Indian-spiced version or pumpkin pie spice to play up the autumn season. You can also add a tiny bit of ground red pepper to any of these flavor combos for a spicy kick. The nuts make a great hostess gift to take to a party or the perfect treat to include in a care package to send during college final exam season.

candied hazelnuts

SERVES **20**   HANDS-ON TIME: **10 MINUTES**   TOTAL TIME: **1 HOUR**

½ cup packed brown sugar
1 large egg white, beaten
½ teaspoon table salt
½ teaspoon vanilla extract
¼ teaspoon ground cinnamon
12 ounces blanched hazelnuts (about 3 cups)

1 Preheat the oven to 250°F.

2 Line a baking sheet with parchment paper.

3 Whisk together the brown sugar, egg white, salt, vanilla, and cinnamon in a large bowl. Add the nuts; toss to coat. Spread the nut mixture in a single layer on the prepared baking sheet. Bake at 250°F until crisp and toasted, about 50 minutes, stirring every 15 minutes. Cool completely. Store the nuts in an airtight container up to 1 week.

prep pointer

Blanching is an easy way to remove the bitter, papery skins from raw hazelnuts before baking. To blanch, boil the nuts along with about 4 tablespoons of baking soda for 3 to 4 minutes. Strain the nuts and place them in a bowl of ice cold water. The skins should come off easily when rubbed.

main dishes

Adding zucchini to traditional shakshuka makes this vegetarian supper super filling. For a tasty twist, serve each portion over a big slice of bread to let the tomato and egg liquid soak into it. You can also save any leftover sauce to top scrambled eggs or toss with pasta.

mixed vegetable shakshuka

SERVES **4**   HANDS-ON TIME: **15 MINUTES**   TOTAL TIME: **58 MINUTES**

2 cups chopped zucchini (from 3 medium zucchini)
1 cup chopped yellow onion (from 1 medium onion)
1 red bell pepper, chopped
1 tablespoon minced garlic (about 3 large garlic cloves)
3 tablespoons olive oil
1 (28-ounce) can diced fire-roasted tomatoes
1 tablespoon tomato paste
1 teaspoon paprika
½ teaspoon ground cumin
¼ teaspoon crushed red pepper
¾ teaspoon table salt
½ teaspoon freshly ground black pepper
6 large eggs
¼ cup chopped fresh flat-leaf parsley

1 Preheat the oven to 375°F.

2 Combine the zucchini, onion, bell pepper, and garlic on a half-sized baking sheet. Drizzle with the oil, and toss to coat. Bake at 375°F until the vegetables are tender and beginning to brown, 20 to 25 minutes, stirring after 15 minutes.

3 Combine the tomatoes, tomato paste, paprika, cumin, red pepper, ½ teaspoon of the salt, and ¼ teaspoon of the black pepper in a large microwave-safe bowl; stir to combine. Microwave at HIGH until hot, 2 to 3 minutes. Pour the tomato mixture over the roasted vegetables; stir to combine. Return to the oven, and roast until the mixture thickens and the tomato liquid is somewhat evaporated, 15 to 20 minutes.

4 Using the back of a spoon, make 6 evenly spaced wells in the vegetable mixture. Break 1 egg into each well; sprinkle the eggs with the remaining ¼ teaspoon each salt and black pepper. Return to the oven, and bake until the eggs reach the desired degree of doneness, 8 to 10 minutes. Sprinkle evenly with the parsley.

prep pointer
Smaller 15-ounce cans of fire-roasted diced tomatoes are more common, so use 2 of them if you cannot find the large can.

For faster prep, microwave the oiled, salted, and fork-pierced potatoes on a microwave-safe plate on HIGH 5 minutes. Flip with a fork, and microwave at HIGH an additional 5 minutes. When done, the potatoes should be tender when pierced with a fork. If the potatoes are not done, microwave at HIGH in 1-minute intervals until fork-tender.

roasted vegetable–loaded potatoes

SERVES **6**   HANDS-ON TIME: **10 MINUTES**   TOTAL TIME: **1 HOUR, 10 MINUTES**

BASIC BAKED POTATOES:

3 large baking potatoes

2 teaspoons vegetable oil

2 teaspoons kosher salt

3 cups chopped fresh cauliflower

2 cups sliced fresh Brussels sprouts

½ medium-sized red onion, sliced

1 tablespoon olive oil

½ teaspoon kosher salt

½ teaspoon freshly ground black pepper

¼ cup golden raisins

¼ cup chopped walnuts, toasted

2 tablespoons bottled lite Italian vinaigrette

1 Make the Basic Baked Potatoes: Preheat the oven to 400°F. Place the potatoes on a lightly greased jelly-roll pan, and drizzle the potatoes with the vegetable oil, and rub with the kosher salt. Pierce the potatoes several times with a fork. Bake at 400°F until tender, about 1 hour.

2 Meanwhile, toss together the cauliflower, Brussels sprouts, onion, olive oil, salt, and pepper in a large bowl. During the last 25 minutes of the potato baking time, add the cauliflower mixture to the pan, spreading it around the potatoes. Return to the oven, and continue baking until the cauliflower is brown (and the potatoes are tender), stirring once, about 25 minutes.

3 Remove the pan from the oven. Cut the potatoes in half. Toss the cauliflower mixture with the raisins, walnuts, and vinaigrette. Spoon the mixture over the potato halves.

Make this filling and delicious meal when you're hungry and time is short. Using microwavable rice is a smart way to streamline cooking so that you're not using more dishes or spending more time in the kitchen than is necessary.

almond AND **rice–stuffed peppers**

SERVES **6**   HANDS-ON TIME: **15 MINUTES**   TOTAL TIME: **1 HOUR, 3 MINUTES**

¼ cup chopped fresh flat-leaf parsley

2 teaspoons finely chopped garlic (from 2 garlic cloves)

2 tablespoons grated lemon rind

3 large red bell peppers

1 (8.8-ounce) pouch microwavable long-grain and wild rice (such as Uncle Ben's)

4 ounces feta cheese, crumbled (about 1 cup)

⅔ cup chopped smoked almonds (about 3½ ounces)

⅔ cup golden raisins

¼ cup chopped scallions (about 6 scallions)

3 tablespoons olive oil

¾ teaspoon table salt

¾ teaspoon freshly ground black pepper

2 tablespoons fresh lemon juice

1 Preheat the oven to 375°F.

2 Stir together the parsley, garlic, and lemon rind in a small bowl.

3 Cut the bell peppers in half lengthwise, leaving the stems intact. Remove and discard the seeds and ribs. Place the bell peppers, cut sides down, on a microwave-safe plate. Microwave at HIGH until slightly softened, 3 to 4 minutes. Place the bell peppers, cut sides up, on a half-sized baking sheet coated with cooking spray.

4 Microwave the rice according to the package directions. Transfer the rice to a medium bowl. Stir in the feta, almonds, raisins, scallions, oil, salt, black pepper, and lemon juice. Divide the rice mixture evenly among the pepper halves. Bake at 375°F until the rice mixture is heated through and the bell peppers are tender, 20 to 25 minutes. Sprinkle with the parsley mixture.

prep pointer

Look for large bell peppers, preferably those with four sides. They will sit flatter than the three-sided ones. In any case, if the bell peppers are falling over when filled, just nestle them close together to keep them from spilling their filling.

Finally, an easy seafood "bake" that lives up to its name. The ridiculously tasty, buttery white wine sauce—kicked up a bit with a little hot sauce and seafood seasoning—is heavenly sopped up with the potatoes or some crusty bread if you have it on hand.

seafood bake WITH buttery wine sauce

SERVES **4**   HANDS-ON TIME: **15 MINUTES**   TOTAL TIME: **40 MINUTES**

12 ounces baby red potatoes (about 11)
2 small yellow onions, cut into 1-inch wedges
2 lemons, halved crosswise
3 tablespoons olive oil
1½ teaspoons Cajun seafood boil seasoning
    (such as Slap Ya Mama Cajun Seafood Boil)
2 pounds littleneck clams in shells, scrubbed
12 ounces smoked andouille sausage, cut into
    2-inch pieces
1 pound fresh mussels in shells, scrubbed
½ cup dry white wine
¼ cup salted butter, melted
1 tablespoon hot sauce (such as Crystal)
1½ teaspoons Worcestershire sauce
2 tablespoons chopped fresh flat-leaf parsley
Lemon wedges, for serving

1 Preheat the oven to 450°F with 1 rack in the top third of the oven and 1 rack in the bottom third of the oven.

2 Toss together the potatoes, onions, lemon halves, oil, and seafood boil seasoning on an aluminum foil–lined baking sheet. Spread in an even layer, and bake at 450°F on the bottom rack until the potatoes are just tender, about 25 minutes.

3 Spread the clams on a second aluminum foil–lined baking sheet. Bake at 450°F on the top rack just until the clams begin to open, about 7 to 9 minutes.

4 When the potatoes have roasted 25 minutes and the clams have opened, spread the andouille evenly on the baking sheet with the potatoes, and spread the mussels evenly over the clams. Pour the wine over the clam mixture. Bake until the mussels have opened, about 8 minutes. Discard any unopened clam or mussel shells.

5 Stir together the butter, hot sauce, and Worcestershire sauce. Spread the potato mixture evenly over the clams and mussels on the baking sheet. Drizzle evenly with the butter sauce, and sprinkle evenly with the parsley. Serve immediately with the lemon wedges.

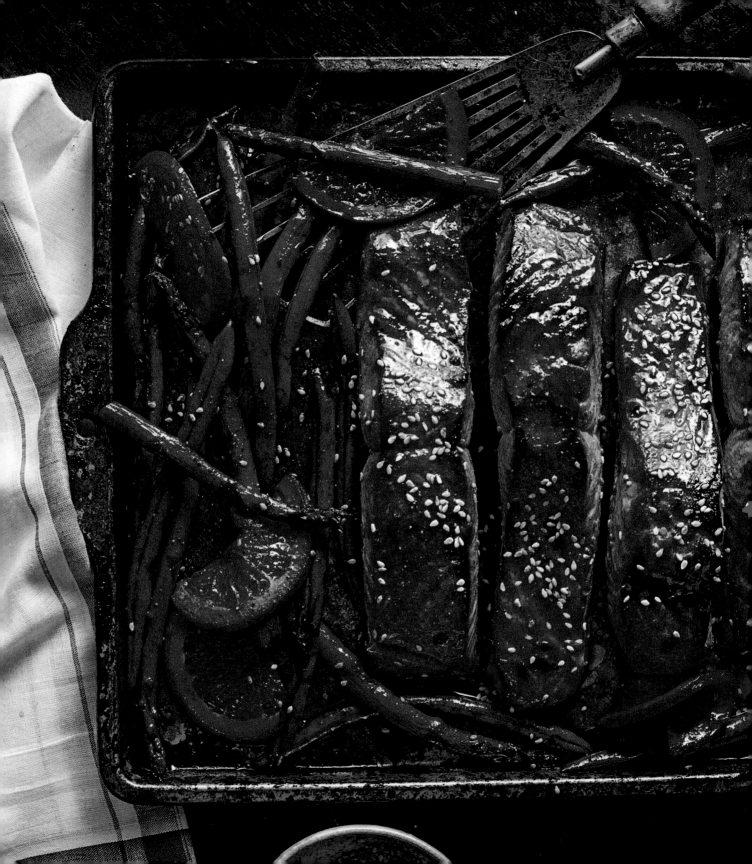

Here's the delicious proof that you can serve a complete, no-mess fish dinner in 25 minutes.

honey-soy glazed salmon WITH veggies AND oranges

SERVES **4**   HANDS-ON TIME: **25 MINUTES**   TOTAL TIME: **25 MINUTES**

4 tablespoons honey
1 tablespoon soy sauce
1 tablespoon Dijon mustard
1 teaspoon seasoned rice wine vinegar
¼ teaspoon dried crushed red pepper
1 pound fresh medium-sized asparagus
8 ounces fresh green beans, trimmed
1 small orange, cut into ¼- to ½-inch slices
1 tablespoon olive oil
1 teaspoon kosher salt
¼ teaspoon freshly ground black pepper
4 (5- to 6-ounce) skinless salmon fillets
Toasted sesame seeds (optional)

1 Preheat the broiler with the oven rack 6 inches from the heat. Whisk together the honey, soy sauce, mustard, rice wine vinegar, and red pepper in a small bowl.

2 Snap off and discard the tough ends of the asparagus. Place the asparagus, green beans, orange slices, olive oil, salt, and pepper in a large bowl, and toss to coat.

3 Place the salmon in the center of a heavy-duty aluminum foil–lined baking sheet. Brush the salmon with about 2 tablespoons of the honey mixture. Spread the asparagus mixture around the salmon.

4 Broil 4 minutes; remove from the oven, and brush the salmon with about 2 tablespoons of the honey mixture. Return to the oven, and broil 4 more minutes. Remove from the oven, and brush the salmon with the remaining honey mixture. Return to the oven, and broil 2 more minutes. Garnish with the sesame seeds, if desired. Serve immediately.

To make this satisfying and speedy dinner for four, you'll only need a few pantry-staple ingredients in addition to the fish, veggies, and potatoes. To amp up the flavor, serve with store-bought tzatziki sauce.

salmon, green beans, AND potatoes

SERVES **4**   HANDS-ON TIME: **20 MINUTES**   TOTAL TIME: **50 MINUTES**

1 pound baby red potatoes (about 15), halved
2 tablespoons extra-virgin olive oil
¾ teaspoon kosher salt
¾ teaspoon freshly ground black pepper
1 pound fresh green beans, trimmed
4 (5- to 6-ounce) skinless salmon fillets
1 lemon, halved

1 Preheat the oven to 425°F.

2 Place the potatoes on a large, half-sized aluminum foil–lined baking sheet. Drizzle with 1 tablespoon of the olive oil and sprinkle with ¼ teaspoon each of the salt and pepper; toss to coat. Arrange the potatoes, cut sides down, and bake at 425°F until the potatoes are fork-tender, 20 to 25 minutes.

3 During the last few minutes of the potato cooking time, place the green beans in a large bowl. Drizzle with the remaining 1 tablespoon olive oil and sprinkle with ¼ teaspoon each of the salt and pepper; toss to coat.

4 Remove the potatoes from the oven. Preheat the broiler.

5 Season the salmon with the remaining ¼ teaspoon each of the salt and pepper. Carefully place the salmon in the center of the baking sheet, and arrange the potatoes and green beans in a single layer around the salmon.

6 Squeeze the lemon halves over the salmon and vegetables. Slice the lemon halves and add to the baking sheet, if desired.

7 Broil the salmon, green beans, potatoes, and lemons until the salmon is no longer translucent but still moist in the center and the green beans, potatoes, and lemons are lightly browned, about 10 minutes.

For a quick weeknight meal that's ready in 40 minutes, serve this flavorful, family-favorite dish. Try the savory-sweet sauce drizzled over any variety of meaty fish.

quick broiled salmon WITH vegetables

SERVES **4**　HAND-ON TIME: **20 MINUTES**　TOTAL TIME: **40 MINUTES**

4 (6-ounce) skin-on salmon fillets

⅜ teaspoon kosher salt

½ teaspoon freshly ground black pepper

1 cup sliced red bell pepper (from 1 large bell pepper)

1 cup vertically sliced onion (from 1½ onions)

1 cup snow peas, trimmed

2 tablespoons rice vinegar

2 tablespoons soy sauce

1½ tablespoons honey

1 tablespoon water

2 teaspoons canola oil

2 teaspoons sambal oelek (ground fresh chile paste)

½ teaspoon cornstarch

3 garlic cloves, sliced

2 (½-inch) pieces peeled fresh ginger

1 Preheat the broiler to high.

2 Place a jelly-roll pan in the oven; preheat the pan for 5 minutes. Sprinkle the salmon fillets evenly with ¼ teaspoon each of the salt and black pepper. Arrange the fillets, skin sides down, on the pan. Broil the fish 5 minutes.

3 Combine the remaining ⅛ teaspoon salt, remaining ¼ teaspoon black pepper, bell pepper, onion, snow peas, and 1 tablespoon of the vinegar in a medium bowl. Arrange the bell pepper mixture on the pan with the fish; broil 3 minutes.

4 Combine the remaining 1 tablespoon vinegar and the remaining ingredients in a microwave-safe bowl. Microwave at HIGH 2 minutes. Stir; let stand 5 minutes. Discard the ginger pieces. Serve the sauce with the fish and vegetables.

A bed of fragrant fresh thyme lends wonderful flavor to this salmon. Choose a fillet cut toward the head end of the fish, and have your fishmonger remove the pin bones.

roasted salmon WITH thyme AND honey-mustard glaze

SERVES **8**   HANDS-ON TIME: **10 MINUTES**   TOTAL TIME: **36 MINUTES**

10 thyme sprigs
1 (3-pound) skin-on salmon fillet, pin bones removed
¼ cup country Dijon mustard
2 tablespoons honey
1 teaspoon white wine vinegar
2 teaspoons fresh thyme leaves
1 teaspoon kosher salt
½ teaspoon freshly ground black pepper
1 lemon, thinly sliced

1 Preheat the oven to 450°F.

2 Line a baking sheet with parchment paper. Arrange the thyme sprigs in a long row on the parchment. Place the salmon, skin side down, on top of the thyme sprigs.

3 Combine the mustard, honey, and vinegar in a bowl. Brush the mixture evenly over the top of the salmon. Sprinkle the salmon with the thyme leaves, salt, and pepper. Arrange the lemon slices over the salmon.

4 Bake the salmon at 450°F in the center of the oven until the desired degree of doneness, 26 minutes. Serve hot or at room temperature.

Place squares of foil on the countertop, and set up an assembly line with the veggies so everyone can fix their own packet. Top each square with a salmon fillet, seal, and bake. When time's up, you can either remove the baked fish and veggies from the packets to plates or let everyone eat right from the foil.

salmon packets

SERVES **4**   HANDS-ON TIME: **15 MINUTES**   TOTAL TIME: **30 MINUTES**

1¾ cups sliced zucchini (from 2 medium zucchini)
1 cup red bell pepper strips
8 lemon slices
4 (6-ounce) skinless salmon fillets
2 tablespoons butter, cut into 4 equal pieces
4 dill sprigs
½ teaspoon kosher salt
½ teaspoon freshly ground black pepper

1 Preheat the oven to 400°F.

2 Cut 4 (14-inch) squares of aluminum foil. Place the zucchini, red bell pepper, and lemon slices in the center of the foil squares. Top each with a salmon fillet, 1 piece of butter, and 1 dill sprig; sprinkle evenly with the salt and pepper. Fold the foil over the fish and vegetables; tightly seal the edges.

3 Place the foil packets on a jelly-roll pan. Bake at 400°F until the fish flakes easily when tested with a fork or until the desired degree of doneness, about 15 to 20 minutes. Remove from the oven; cut open the packets and serve.

For even easier prep, make the lime mayonnaise (Step 2) ahead of time and store it in an airtight container in the refrigerator until ready to use, up to two days.

tilapia tacos

SERVES **4**   HANDS-ON TIME: **19 MINUTES**   TOTAL TIME: **28 MINUTES**

½ cup sliced green onions

¼ cup chopped fresh cilantro, plus more for garnish (optional)

3 tablespoons canola mayonnaise

3 tablespoons sour cream

1 teaspoon grated lime rind

1½ teaspoons fresh lime juice

⅜ teaspoon table salt

1 garlic clove, minced

1 teaspoon ground cumin

1 teaspoon ground coriander

½ teaspoon Spanish smoked paprika

¼ teaspoon ground red pepper

⅛ teaspoon garlic powder

1½ pounds tilapia fillets (4 to 6 fillets)

8 (6-inch) corn tortillas

2 cups angel hair slaw

1 cup chopped tomatoes

½ cup sliced red onion

8 lime wedges (from 2 limes)

1 Preheat the oven to 425°F.

2 Combine ¼ cup each of the green onion and cilantro, the mayonnaise, sour cream, lime rind, lime juice, ½ teaspoon of the salt, and garlic in a small bowl; stir well. Cover and chill until ready to serve.

3 Combine the cumin, coriander, paprika, red pepper, garlic powder, and the remaining ⅛ teaspoon salt in a small bowl; sprinkle the spice mixture over both sides of the fillets. Place the fillets on a baking sheet coated with cooking spray. Bake at 425°F until the fish flakes easily when tested with a fork, about 9 to 10 minutes. Cool slightly. Place the fish in a large bowl; break into pieces with a fork.

4 Warm the tortillas according to the package directions. Place 2 tortillas on each of 4 plates. Evenly divide the slaw and fish among the tortillas. Top each tortilla with the tomato, red onion, remaining green onions, and the lime-mayonnaise mixture. Garnish with cilantro, if desired. Serve with the lime wedges.

Wrapping the food in foil allows the fish to cook without losing any moisture and the veggies to steam just until crisp-tender. Serve with precooked microwavable brown rice to catch all the sesame, lime, and soy goodness in each packet. Make sure to crimp the edges of the packets well so no steam or juices escape during cooking.

foil-wrapped sesame-soy tilapia

SERVES **4**   HANDS-ON TIME: **10 MINUTES**   TOTAL TIME: **30 MINUTES**

5 cups thinly sliced napa (Chinese) cabbage (from 1 medium cabbage)

1 cup matchstick-cut carrots (about 2 medium carrots)

1 cup snow peas

1 medium-sized red bell pepper, thinly sliced

2 tablespoons toasted sesame oil

1 tablespoon fresh lime juice

4 (5-ounce) tilapia fillets

8 teaspoons soy sauce

¼ teaspoon kosher salt

¼ teaspoon freshly ground black pepper

2 teaspoons sesame seeds, toasted (optional)

4 lime wedges

1 Preheat the oven to 400°F.

2 Combine the cabbage, carrots, snow peas, and bell pepper in a bowl; toss. Combine the oil and juice in a bowl. Add the oil mixture to the cabbage mixture; toss.

3 Divide the cabbage mixture evenly among 4 (14-inch) squares of aluminum foil; top with the fillets. Drizzle 2 teaspoons of the soy sauce over each fillet; sprinkle evenly with the salt and black pepper.

4 Bring the edges of the foil up over the fillets; fold to seal. Place, seal sides up, on a baking sheet. Bake at 400°F for 20 minutes. Open the packets; sprinkle with the sesame seeds, if desired. Serve with the lime wedges.

prep pointer

You can substitute salmon for the tilapia and small broccoli or cauliflower florets, sliced zucchini, or asparagus for any of the vegetables.

Kids and parents alike will love this fresh take on nuggets and fries. The panko-dredged fish pieces and the asparagus bake together on the same baking sheet for a simple and quick meal.

fish nuggets WITH crispy asparagus "fries"

SERVES **4**   HANDS-ON TIME: **20 MINUTES**   TOTAL TIME: **32 MINUTES**

1 pound tilapia fillets
⅜ teaspoon table salt
¼ teaspoon freshly ground black pepper
⅓ cup cornstarch
1 tablespoon water
1 large egg
1 cup whole-wheat panko (Japanese breadcrumbs)
2 tablespoons canola oil
1 pound asparagus, trimmed
¼ cup canola mayonnaise
1 tablespoon dill pickle relish
1 tablespoon finely chopped green onions

1 Preheat the oven to 450°F.

2 Place a large baking sheet in the oven (leave the baking sheet in the oven as it preheats). Cut the fish into 1½-inch pieces; sprinkle evenly with ¼ teaspoon each of the salt and pepper. Place the cornstarch in a shallow dish (such as a pie plate).

3 Combine the water and egg in a shallow bowl; stir with a fork. Place the panko in a shallow dish. Dredge the fish in the cornstarch; shake off the excess. Dip the fish in the egg mixture. Dredge in the panko. Carefully remove the baking sheet from the oven; coat with cooking spray. Drizzle the oil over the baking sheet; tilt to coat with the oil.

4 Arrange the asparagus on one side of the baking sheet and the fish on the other. Sprinkle the asparagus with the remaining ⅛ teaspoon salt. Bake at 450°F until done, about 12 minutes, turning the fish and stirring the asparagus after 8 minutes. Combine the mayonnaise, relish, and onions in a small bowl. Arrange the fish and the asparagus on each of 4 plates. Serve with the sauce.

This supereasy and fast-to-make catfish slathered in a spicy Greek yogurt–soy nut mixture makes a satisfying entrée. For a quick side, add peeled sweet potatoes cut into ¼- to ½-inch thick sticks, to the baking sheet and bake for an additional 10 minutes after removing the fish.

soy nut–crusted catfish

SERVES **4**   HANDS-ON TIME: **8 MINUTES**   TOTAL TIME: **20 MINUTES**

½ cup salted roasted soy nuts
¼ cup plain Greek yogurt
2 tablespoons fresh lime juice
1 teaspoon Southwest chipotle seasoning
¼ teaspoon table salt
¼ teaspoon freshly ground black pepper
4 (6-ounce) catfish fillets
Fresh parsley leaves (optional)
Lemon wedges

1 Preheat the oven to 400°F.

2 Place the soy nuts in a large heavy-duty zip-top plastic bag; coarsely crush the soy nuts using a rolling pin or meat mallet. Transfer the soy nuts to a shallow dish.

3 Combine the yogurt, lime juice, chipotle seasoning, salt, and pepper in a small bowl. Brush the tops of the fish with the yogurt mixture; dredge in the soy nuts.

4 Place the fish on a baking sheet coated with cooking spray. Bake at 400°F until the fish flakes easily when tested with a fork, 12 minutes. Garnish with parsley, if desired, and serve with the lemon wedges.

flavor note

Soy nuts—dried soybeans that have been soaked, drained, and roasted—have a nutty flavor. You can use them instead of nuts in many recipes.

Who says dinner parties require elaborate preparation? This sea bass, with a beautiful, tangy citrus topping, is an elegant, guest-worthy entrée. While the fish bakes, whip up the salsa and have the dish on the table in just 20 minutes. Serve with a mixed greens salad or our Roasted Red Bliss Potato Salad (page 146), if desired.

sea bass WITH citrus salsa

SERVES **4**   HANDS-ON TIME: **10 MINUTES**   TOTAL TIME: **20 MINUTES**

2½ tablespoons extra-virgin olive oil
¾ teaspoon kosher salt
¾ teaspoon freshly ground black pepper
½ teaspoon paprika
4 (6-ounce) skinless sea bass fillets
1 small pink grapefruit
1 small navel orange
3 tablespoons chopped fresh cilantro
1 tablespoon fresh lime juice
1 teaspoon minced fresh garlic
¼ cup thinly vertically sliced white onion (from 1 onion)
Lime wedges

1 Preheat the broiler to high with the oven rack 6 to 8 inches from the heat.

2 Combine 1½ teaspoons of the oil, ½ teaspoon each of the salt and pepper, and the paprika. Place the fish on a baking sheet; rub with the paprika mixture. Broil the fish until it begins to brown and the fish flakes easily with a fork, 10 to 12 minutes. Keep warm.

3 Meanwhile, peel the grapefruit and orange. Using a small knife, cut the fruit into segments, and coarsely chop. Whisk together the cilantro, lime juice, garlic, remaining 2 tablespoons oil, and remaining ¼ teaspoon each salt and pepper; stir in the onion and citrus segments. Spoon the salsa over the fish. Serve with the lime wedges.

flavor note

Instead of sea bass, you can also use cod, sablefish (also called black cod), striped bass, or barramundi with great results. Any of these white-fleshed fish will take well to the bright flavors of the grapefruit-and-orange topping.

This hearty dinner for four is one you'll want to make all fall and winter.

garlicky roasted spatchcock chicken

SERVES **4**   HANDS-ON TIME: **30 MINUTES**   TOTAL TIME: **1 HOUR, 30 MINUTES**

1 (5-pound) whole chicken

4 garlic cloves, chopped

1 teaspoon kosher salt

6 tablespoons salted butter, softened

1 tablespoon chopped fresh thyme

2 tablespoons lemon rind, plus 3 tablespoons
   fresh juice

¾ teaspoon freshly ground black pepper

12 ounces baby red potatoes (about 11), halved

8 ounces small carrots with tops, trimmed

8 ounces fresh Brussels sprouts, trimmed and halved

1 Preheat the oven to 450°F.

2 Rinse the chicken, and pat dry. Place the chicken, breast side down, on a cutting board. Using poultry shears, cut along both sides of the backbone, and remove the backbone. (Discard or reserve for a stock.) Turn the chicken breast side up, and open the underside of the chicken like a book. Using the heel of your hand, press firmly against the breastbone until it cracks. Place the chicken on a large baking sheet. Tuck the wing tips under the chicken so they don't burn.

3 Combine the garlic and salt on a cutting board. Using the flat edge of a knife, mash into a paste. Combine the garlic paste, butter, thyme, lemon rind, and pepper in a bowl. Set aside 2 tablespoons of the garlic mixture. Rub the remaining garlic mixture under the skin of the chicken breasts and thighs.

4 Bake the chicken at 450°F for 10 minutes. Remove the baking sheet from the oven. Reduce the heat to 400°F. Arrange the potatoes and carrots around the chicken; return to the oven, and bake 20 minutes. Arrange the Brussels sprouts around the chicken, and spread the remaining 2 tablespoons garlic mixture on the breasts; return to the oven, and bake until a meat thermometer inserted in the thickest portion registers 165°F, about 20 minutes. Drizzle with the lemon juice, and let stand 10 minutes. Carve the chicken, and serve with the pan juices and vegetables.

prep pointer

Spatchcocking, also called butterflying, is the technique of removing a chicken's backbone. It ensures juicy meat and golden crisp skin in less time than roasting a whole bird. Although it does require some basic knife skills, it's the fastest way to roast a chicken.

Serve this dish to your family on a busy weeknight. Spend just 10 minutes preparing the food—a balanced meal of meat, vegetables, and rice—and turn to other duties while it cooks. You can even serve the dish straight from the baking sheet to make cleanup even easier.

simple whole chicken WITH roasted broccoli-mushroom rice

SERVES **4 TO 6**   HANDS-ON TIME: **10 MINUTES**   TOTAL TIME: **1 HOUR, 15 MINUTES**

1 (3½- to 4-pound) whole chicken, cut into pieces
⅓ cup olive oil
3 teaspoons kosher salt
2 teaspoons freshly ground black pepper
2 (8.5-ounce) pouches microwavable ready-to-serve rice (such as Uncle Ben's Ready Rice)
1 pound fresh broccoli
2 (8-ounce) packages fresh cremini mushrooms, sliced

1 Preheat the oven to 425°F.

2 Rub the chicken pieces with 1 tablespoon of the olive oil; sprinkle with 2 teaspoons of the salt and 1 teaspoon of the pepper.

3 Spread the ready-to-serve rice in an even layer on a heavy-duty aluminum foil–lined baking sheet, breaking up the clumps.

4 Cut the broccoli into florets. Toss together the broccoli florets, 2 tablespoons of the oil, and ½ teaspoon each of the salt and pepper in a medium bowl; spread in an even layer over the rice. Toss together the mushrooms and the remaining olive oil, salt, and pepper, and spread over the broccoli and rice.

5 Place the chicken pieces, skin sides up, 1½ inches apart on the broccoli and mushrooms.

6 Bake at 425°F until a meat thermometer inserted in the thickest portion of the chicken registers 165°F, about 1 hour. Let stand 5 minutes before serving.

Quarter the chicken yourself by removing each breast first, then the thigh and leg pieces. Or purchase leg quarters and bone-in breasts.

chimichurri roasted chicken WITH potatoes AND onions

SERVES **6**   HANDS-ON TIME: **10 MINUTES**   TOTAL TIME: **55 MINUTES**

½ cup finely chopped shallots (1 large shallot)
⅓ cup chopped fresh cilantro
¼ cup olive oil
¼ cup red wine vinegar
1½ teaspoons kosher salt
¾ teaspoon crushed red pepper
1 (4½-pound) whole chicken, quartered
1 tablespoon paprika
1 pound baby red potatoes (about 15), quartered
2 small red onions, cut into wedges
Cilantro leaves (optional)

1 Preheat the oven to 425°F. Line a baking sheet with aluminum foil.

2 Combine the shallots, cilantro, 2 tablespoons each of the oil and vinegar, 1 teaspoon of the salt, and the red pepper in a small bowl. Carefully remove the skin from the chicken; reserve. Rub the cilantro mixture evenly over the chicken. Arrange the reserved chicken skin over the chicken.

3 Drizzle 1 tablespoon of the oil over the prepared baking sheet. Add the paprika and potatoes; toss to coat. Add the onions to the baking sheet; top with the remaining 1 tablespoon oil and remaining ½ teaspoon salt. Arrange the chicken quarters, skin side up, on the baking sheet. Bake at 425°F until the chicken is done, 35 minutes. Place the chicken on a cutting board; let stand 5 minutes. Remove the skin from the breasts; discard. Cut the breasts in half crosswise.

4 Preheat the broiler to high.

5 Return the vegetables to the oven; broil 5 minutes or until the vegetables are caramelized. Return the chicken to the baking sheet; top with the remaining 2 tablespoons vinegar and cilantro sprigs, if desired.

prep pointer

The skin will help insulate the meat and lock in the chimichurri flavor as it roasts in the hot oven. It's easiest to remove the skin, and then replace it after rubbing the herb mixture over the chicken.

Any leftovers of this supersatisfying salad are great to pack up for a next-day lunch, as the heartier greens are less prone to wilting quickly. Use the reserved chicken for Greek Chicken Nachos (page 87).

garlic-sage roasted chicken WITH kale AND radicchio caesar salad

SERVES **4**   HANDS-ON TIME: **30 MINUTES**   TOTAL TIME: **1 HOUR, 20 MINUTES**

2 (3½-pound) whole chickens
1½ tablespoons olive oil
2 tablespoons minced fresh sage
1 tablespoon grated lemon rind
1¼ teaspoons freshly ground black pepper
1 teaspoon kosher salt
3 garlic cloves, minced
¾ cup plus 2 tablespoons hot water
2 tablespoons canola mayonnaise
1 tablespoon fresh lemon juice
½ teaspoon anchovy paste
½ cup very thinly sliced radicchio
5 ounces fresh baby kale
1 ounce Parmesan cheese, shaved (about ¼ cup)

1 Preheat the oven to 450°F.

2 Line a baking sheet with foil; place a wire rack on the baking sheet. Coat the rack with cooking spray. Place 1 chicken, breast side down, on a cutting board. Using kitchen shears, cut along either side of the backbone; discard the bone. Turn the chicken over; press down on the thighs and wings with the heel of your hand. Arrange the chicken, breast side up, on the rack. Repeat the procedure with the remaining chicken.

3 Starting at the neck of 1 chicken, loosen the skin from the breasts and drumsticks by inserting fingers, gently pushing between the skin and meat. Combine the oil, sage, lemon rind, ½ teaspoon each of the pepper and salt, and the garlic in a bowl. Rub the sage mixture under the loosened skin, over the meat. (Do not season the other chicken.) Add ¾ cup of water to the baking sheet. Bake the chickens at 450°F until a thermometer inserted into the thickest part of the thigh registers 165°F, 40 minutes. Let stand 10 minutes. Remove the skin from both chickens; discard. Sprinkle the unseasoned chicken with ½ teaspoon of the pepper and the remaining ½ teaspoon salt. Carve both chickens. When cool, shred the unseasoned chicken, keeping the light and dark meat separate. Reserve the shredded chicken for another use.

4 Combine the remaining ¼ teaspoon pepper, remaining 2 tablespoons hot water, mayonnaise, juice, and anchovy paste in a large bowl. Add the radicchio and kale; toss. Sprinkle with the Parmesan. Serve with the garlic-sage chicken.

This gorgeous dish—pictured on the cover—is as satisfying as it is simple to prepare. It is sure to become a go-to meal at your table.

roasted rosemary chicken quarters WITH butternut squash AND brussels sprouts

SERVES **4**   HANDS-ON TIME: **18 MINUTES**   TOTAL TIME: **1 HOUR, 8 MINUTES**

4 skin-on, bone-in chicken leg quarters
  (3½ to 4 pounds total)
3 tablespoons olive oil
1¾ teaspoons kosher salt
1½ teaspoons freshly ground black pepper
3 cups cubed butternut squash (about 1-inch pieces)
  (1 [12-ounce] package or 1 large squash)
1 pound Brussels sprouts, trimmed and halved
1 medium-sized red onion, cut into thin wedges
10 whole garlic cloves
1 tablespoon honey
½ teaspoon Dijon mustard
1 to 2 tablespoons chopped fresh rosemary

1 Preheat the oven to 425°F.

2 Place a large baking sheet coated with cooking spray in the oven; heat 5 minutes.

3 Brush the chicken with 1 tablespoon of the oil; sprinkle with ¾ teaspoon each of the salt and pepper. Remove the baking sheet from the oven, and place the chicken quarters, skin side down, on the baking sheet; return to the oven. Bake at 425°F for 10 minutes.

4 Remove the baking sheet from the oven; add the butternut squash, Brussels sprouts, onion, and garlic; drizzle with 1½ tablespoons of the olive oil, and sprinkle with the remaining salt and pepper. Toss well.

5 Place the chicken over the vegetables. Combine the remaining ½ tablespoon oil, honey, and Dijon mustard; brush onto the chicken using a pastry brush.

6 Bake at 425°F for 15 minutes. Baste the vegetables and chicken thighs with the pan juices using a large spoon or bulb baster; sprinkle with the rosemary. Bake 20 more minutes or until the chicken is done, shielding the chicken during the last 5 minutes, if needed, to prevent over browning.

If you want extra browning, pop the baking sheet under the broiler for about 5 minutes, being careful not to let the vegetables get too dark.

sumac chicken WITH cauliflower AND carrots

SERVES **6**   HANDS-ON TIME: **10 MINUTES**   TOTAL TIME: **50 MINUTES**

6 tablespoons olive oil

1 tablespoon sumac

1¼ teaspoons kosher salt

1 teaspoon light brown sugar

1 teaspoon paprika

¼ teaspoon ground red pepper

1 pound cauliflower florets

2 (6-ounce) packages small rainbow carrots, halved lengthwise

1 pound skinless, bone-in chicken thighs

1 pound skinless drumsticks

1 small lemon, halved lengthwise and thinly sliced

1 small red onion, cut into ¾-inch wedges

½ cup finely chopped fresh flat-leaf parsley

½ cup chopped fresh cilantro

1 tablespoon fresh lemon juice

1 small garlic clove

1 Preheat the oven to 425°F.

2 Combine 3 tablespoons of the oil, the sumac, 1 teaspoon of the salt, the brown sugar, paprika, and red pepper in a medium bowl. Place the cauliflower and carrots on an aluminum foil–lined baking sheet. Add half of the oil mixture; toss to coat. Add the chicken thighs, drumsticks, and lemon slices to the baking sheet. Rub the remaining oil mixture over the chicken. Bake at 425°F for 20 minutes. Stir the vegetables. Sprinkle the onion wedges over the chicken and vegetables. Bake at 425°F until the chicken is done, 20 more minutes.

3 Combine the remaining 3 tablespoons oil, parsley, cilantro, lemon juice, and garlic in a small bowl. Spoon the parsley mixture evenly over the chicken and vegetables. Sprinkle with the remaining ¼ teaspoon salt.

flavor note

Sumac has a tart, lemony quality. It's fantastic as a rub here, but is also delicious in vinaigrettes or sprinkled over dips. If you can't find sumac, you can substitute 1 teaspoon grated lemon rind.

Enough protein, starch, and vegetables go onto the baking sheet to make this recipe a well-rounded meal.

chicken WITH potatoes AND carrots

SERVES **6 TO 8**   HANDS-ON TIME: **15 MINUTES**   TOTAL TIME: **1 HOUR, 10 MINUTES**

8 skin-on, bone-in chicken thighs (about 4 pounds)
2 tablespoons olive oil
2 teaspoons kosher salt
1 teaspoon freshly ground black pepper
1 teaspoon finely chopped fresh rosemary
1 (24-ounce) package fingerling potatoes, halved
8 ounces small carrots with tops
1 large sweet onion, cut into 8 wedges

1 Preheat the oven to 375°F.

2 Rub the chicken thighs evenly with 1 tablespoon of the olive oil. Stir together the salt, pepper, and rosemary in a small bowl. Sprinkle the chicken thighs evenly with 3 teaspoons of the salt mixture.

3 Stir together the potatoes, carrots, and onion in a large bowl. Drizzle with the remaining 1 tablespoon olive oil, and sprinkle with the remaining 1 teaspoon salt mixture; toss to coat.

4 Spread the potato mixture in a even layer on a heavy-duty aluminum foil–lined baking sheet lightly greased with cooking spray. Place the chicken thighs 2 to 3 inches apart on top of the potato mixture.

5 Bake at 375°F until a meat thermometer inserted in the thickest portion of the chicken registers 165°F, about 55 minutes to 1 hour.

prep pointer

The trick to extra savory veggies is cooking the chicken atop the potatoes, carrots, and onion.

Chinese five-spice is a seasoning blend used in many Chinese dishes. Here, it adds warmth and sweetness to the dish without making it too sweet, as the apples are tart enough to balance the flavor.

five-spice chicken thighs WITH apples AND sweet potatoes

SERVES **4 TO 6**   HANDS-ON TIME: **35 MINUTES**   TOTAL TIME: **1 HOUR, 5 MINUTES**

1 small fennel bulb with feathery stalks

¾ pound sweet potatoes, peeled and cut into ¼-inch slices

1¼ teaspoons kosher salt

½ teaspoon freshly ground black pepper

1 medium-sized red onion, cut lengthwise into ⅓-inch-wide slices

2 large firm-tart apples, such as Ida Red, Sierra Beauty, or Granny Smith, unpeeled, sliced into ¼-inch wedges

6 skin-on, bone-in chicken thighs (2¾ pounds)

2 tablespoons salted butter, melted

1 teaspoon honey

1½ teaspoons Chinese five-spice

1 Preheat the oven to 425°F.

2 Cut off the fennel stalks and reserve the feathery leaves. Trim the base of the bulb and any tough outer layers. Halve the bulb lengthwise, cut out the core in a V, and cut the bulb lengthwise into slim wedges.

3 Coat a large baking sheet with cooking spray. Arrange the sweet potatoes and fennel in a single layer on the baking sheet. Sprinkle with ½ teaspoon of the salt and ¼ teaspoon of the pepper. Arrange the onion and apples over the potatoes and sprinkle with ¼ teaspoon of the salt and the remaining ¼ teaspoon pepper. Set the chicken on top. Combine the butter, honey, five-spice, and the remaining ½ teaspoon salt in a small bowl. Brush onto the chicken.

4 Bake at 425°F for 15 minutes. Baste the ingredients with the pan juices using a bulb baster or wide spoon. Continue baking until the chicken is browned and no longer pink at the bone, 15 to 20 minutes. Baste everything again, and scatter the reserved fennel leaves on top.

flavor note

Head to your farmers' market between August and November for the freshest, ripest apples that will yield the most flavorful, sweetest results.

Sticky-sweet chicken thighs are only a few simple steps away with this recipe. Pair the thighs with Roasted Winter Vegetables with Miso Vinaigrette (page 149) for a satisfying, Asian-inspired meal.

glazed roasted chicken thighs

SERVES **2**   HANDS-ON TIME: **10 MINUTES**   TOTAL TIME: **8 HOURS, 40 MINUTES, INCLUDES CHILLING**

¼ cup teriyaki sauce

2 tablespoons frozen orange juice concentrate, thawed

1½ tablespoons dark sesame oil

2 garlic cloves, minced

½ teaspoon table salt

¼ teaspoon freshly ground black pepper

4 skinless, bone-in chicken thighs (about 1¼ pounds)

½ teaspoon sesame seeds

1 Stir together the teriyaki sauce, orange juice concentrate, sesame oil, garlic, salt, and pepper in a bowl. Reserve half of the teriyaki sauce mixture; store in an airtight container in the refrigerator up to 2 days.

2 Pour the remaining mixture into a large shallow dish or zip-top plastic freezer bag; add the chicken. Cover or seal, and chill 8 hours, turning occasionally.

3 Preheat the oven to 450°F.

4 Remove the chicken from the marinade; discarde the marinade. Place the chicken on an aluminum foil–lined jelly-roll pan.

5 Bake at 450°F until a meat thermometer inserted in the thickest portion of the chicken registers 165°F, 30 minutes, basting once with the reserved teriyaki sauce mixture. Skim the fat from the pan juices; stir the remaining juices into the reserved teriyaki sauce mixture. Brush the chicken with the mixture. Sprinkle with the sesame seeds. Serve immediately.

flavor note

Dark sesame oil differs from regular sesame oil in that the dark variety is made with toasted sesame seeds, which gives it its rich brown color. Dark sesame oil also has a much stronger sesame flavor than the regular kind does.

Crispy, crunchy chicken drizzled with a spicy honey-mustard sauce is soon to become a favorite chicken dish. Baking the chicken provides a satisfying crunch without the added fat from frying. Serve with Orange, Honey, and Thyme Biscuits (page 198) and microwave-steamed broccoli for a complete meal.

honey-pecan chicken thighs

SERVES **4**   HANDS-ON TIME: **20 MINUTES**   TOTAL TIME: **3 HOURS, INCLUDES CHILLING**

8 skinless, boneless chicken thighs (about 1⅓ pounds)
½ teaspoon table salt
½ teaspoon freshly ground black pepper
½ teaspoon ground red pepper
½ teaspoon dried thyme
¾ cup honey
¾ cup Dijon mustard
2 garlic cloves, minced
1 cup finely chopped pecans
½ teaspoon curry powder
Italian parsley sprigs (optional)

1 Line a baking sheet with aluminum foil; place a wire rack on the baking sheet.

2 Place the chicken in a shallow dish. Combine the salt, black pepper, red pepper, and thyme in a small bowl; sprinkle evenly over the chicken. Stir together ½ cup each of the honey and mustard, and the garlic; pour over the chicken. Cover and chill 2 hours.

3 Preheat the oven to 375°F.

4 Remove the chicken from the marinade; discard the marinade. Place the pecans in a shallow dish. Dredge the chicken in the pecans; place on the wire rack on the baking sheet.

5 Bake at 375°F until a meat thermometer inserted into the thickest portion of the chicken registers 165°F, 40 minutes.

6 Meanwhile, stir together the remaining ¼ cup each honey and mustard and the curry powder; serve the sauce with the chicken. Garnish with the parsley sprigs, if desired.

Dinner doesn't get much easier, or more fun, than baking-sheet nachos. The baking sheet does double duty: Toast the chips first, and then pile them high with toppings and return to the oven to melt the cheese and heat everything through. Here, the Mexican classic takes a detour to Greece with pita chips, a shredded Greek salad, and crumbled feta. Rotisserie chicken breast makes this meal even easier, though this dish is a great use for any leftover cooked chicken, such as the reserved shredded chicken from Garlic-Sage Roasted Chicken (page 76). Bring the whole baking sheet to the table and cut into servings, like you would a square pizza.

greek chicken nachos

SERVES **6**   HANDS-ON TIME: **24 MINUTES**   TOTAL TIME: **53 MINUTES**

3 (6-inch) whole-wheat pitas
Cooking spray
2½ tablespoons extra-virgin olive oil
2 tablespoons red wine vinegar
¼ teaspoon freshly ground black pepper
4 cups shredded romaine lettuce
1 cup grape tomatoes, halved lengthwise
1 cup chopped English cucumber
10 pitted kalamata olives, halved lengthwise
8 ounces skinless, boneless rotisserie chicken breast, shredded (about 2 cups)
3 ounces part-skim mozzarella cheese, shredded (about ¾ cup)
2 ounces feta cheese, crumbled (about ½ cup)
2 tablespoons coarsely chopped fresh oregano

1 Preheat the oven to 400°F.

2 Split each pita in half horizontally into rounds. Coat the cut sides of the pitas with cooking spray. Cut each pita half into 8 wedges. Arrange half of the wedges, cut sides up, on an aluminum foil-lined baking sheet. Bake at 400°F until browned, 8 minutes; remove from the baking sheet. Repeat the procedure with the remaining wedges. Cool 10 minutes.

3 Combine the oil, vinegar, and pepper in a medium bowl, stirring with a whisk. Add the lettuce, tomatoes, cucumber, and olives; toss to coat.

4 Arrange all the pita chips on the foil-lined baking sheet so they overlap. Top with the chicken, mozzarella, and feta. Bake at 400°F for 3 minutes or until the mozzarella melts. Top with the lettuce mixture and oregano.

main dishes

Use 1 reserved dough portion to make Zucchini-Ricotta Pizza
(page 178), and freeze the other reserved portion for up to 3 months.

broccoli, cheddar, AND chicken calzones

SERVES **4**   HANDS-ON TIME: **16 MINUTES**   TOTAL TIME: **2 HOURS, 36 MINUTES**

PIZZA DOUGH:

2 cups warm water (100° to 110°F)

3½ teaspoons dry yeast

2 teaspoons sugar

2 tablespoons olive oil

1½ teaspoons kosher salt

1 teaspoon freshly ground black pepper

23.75 ounces white whole-wheat flour (about 5 cups)

⅓ cup buttermilk

2 tablespoons minced fresh chives

2 tablespoons canola mayonnaise

1 tablespoon chopped fresh dill

1 tablespoon cider vinegar

½ teaspoon freshly ground black pepper

¼ teaspoon crushed red pepper

⅛ teaspoon kosher salt

2 garlic cloves, grated

2 cups small broccoli florets (from 1 head)

6 ounces skinless, boneless rotisserie chicken,
   shredded (about 1½ cups)

4 ounces colby-Jack cheese, shredded (about 1 cup)

1 large egg, lightly beaten

1 Make the Pizza Dough: Place the warm water, yeast, and sugar in a stand mixer fitted with a dough hook; let stand 5 minutes. Stir in the olive oil, 1¼ teaspoons of the salt, and black pepper. Weigh or lightly spoon the flour into dry measuring cups; level with a knife. Add the flour to the bowl; beat at low speed just until combined.

2 Cover; let stand 20 minutes. Uncover; beat at medium-low speed 8 minutes. Turn the dough out onto a work surface. Knead 1 minute; form into a ball. Place in a bowl coated with cooking spray; turn to coat. Cover and let rise in a warm place (85°F), free from drafts, about 1 hour. Punch the dough down. Divide into 3 portions. Wrap 2 portions in plastic wrap; reserve for another use. Cover the remaining dough portion; let rise 30 minutes.

3 Preheat the oven to 450°F. Line a baking sheet with parchment paper. Cut the dough into 4 equal portions; cover and let stand 10 minutes.

4 Combine the buttermilk and next 8 ingredients (through grated garlic). Steam the broccoli 1 minute. Rinse with cold water; drain. Combine the broccoli, buttermilk mixture, chicken, and colby-Jack in a large bowl.

5 Roll each dough portion into a 6½-inch circle. Place about 1 cup of the filling slightly off-center on each. Fold the dough over the filling; crimp the edges to seal. Place on the baking sheet. Bake at 450°F for 10 minutes. Brush with the egg; bake at 450°F for 10 minutes.

A perfect dinner for those nights when time is short and appetites are huge—also known as any weeknight—this easy meal comes together in under an hour, uses a handful of ingredients, and cooks on a single baking sheet, including the rice.

chicken sausage WITH fennel AND apples

SERVES **4**   HANDS-ON TIME: **10 MINUTES**   TOTAL TIME: **50 MINUTES**

6 tablespoons olive oil

¼ cup apple cider vinegar

1 teaspoon kosher salt

¾ teaspoon freshly ground black pepper

1 pound Italian chicken sausage links

2 small fennel bulbs, sliced, fronds reserved

2 medium-sized Honeycrisp apples, cut into 1-inch wedges

2 (8.8-ounce) pouches microwavable ready-to-serve rice (such as Uncle Ben's Ready Rice)

1 Preheat the oven to 375°F.

2 Whisk together the oil, vinegar, salt, and pepper in a small bowl. Toss together the sausages, fennel, apples, and 6 tablespoons of the vinegar mixture in a large bowl. Reserve the remaining vinegar mixture.

3 Place the rice in a mound in the center of a lightly greased large baking sheet. Place the sausages, fennel, and apples over the rice, covering it completely, and drizzle with any remaining vinegar. Bake at 375°F until the sausages are cooked through and the fennel and apples are golden, about 40 minutes.

4 Chop the reserved fennel fronds to equal 1 tablespoon. Divide the vegetables, rice, and sausages evenly among 4 plates. Drizzle with the reserved vinegar mixture, and sprinkle evenly with the chopped fennel fronds.

flavor note

Crisp and slightly sweet, fennel caramelizes beautifully when roasted in the oven. Be sure to reserve a few of the soft green fennel fronds to top the finished dish for a pretty bit of green and more delicious fennel flavor.

It doesn't have to be Thanksgiving to cook an amazing turkey dish, though this recipe is certainly holiday-dinner worthy. The cabbage and sweet potatoes cook right alongside the poultry, making prep super simple.

bavarian turkey tenderloin WITH caraway sweet potatoes AND cabbage salad

SERVES **4**   HANDS-ON TIME: **10 MINUTES**   TOTAL TIME: **40 MINUTES**

1 pound green cabbage (from 1 small head cabbage), cut into 1-inch pieces

½ pound sweet potatoes, peeled and chopped

1 teaspoon caraway seeds

7 tablespoons olive oil

1½ teaspoons table salt

1 teaspoon freshly ground black pepper

1 teaspoon dry mustard

½ teaspoon ground cinnamon

¼ teaspoon ground ginger

¼ teaspoon ground cloves

1¼ pounds turkey tenderloins (about 2 tenderloins)

1 Preheat the oven to 425°F.

2 Combine the cabbage, potatoes, caraway seeds, ¼ cup of the oil, 1 teaspoon of the salt, and ½ teaspoon of the pepper in a large bowl; toss to coat. Arrange the mixture in an even layer on a half-sized baking sheet.

3 Stir together the dry mustard, cinnamon, ginger, cloves, remaining 3 tablespoons oil, and ½ teaspoon each salt and pepper in a small bowl. Rub the mixture evenly over the tenderloins. Place the tenderloins on the vegetable mixture in the middle of the baking sheet. Bake at 425°F until the vegetables are tender and a meat thermometer inserted in the thickest portion of the tenderloins registers 165°F, 25 to 30 minutes. Let the turkey stand 5 minutes before slicing.

prep pointer

If you don't have sweet potatoes, substitute chopped carrots or butternut squash.

Make a restaurant-quality dinner in your own kitchen with this fantastic recipe. The green beans and multi-colored grape tomatoes give this dish a gorgeous presentation that will wow your guests.

rib-eyes WITH veggies AND blue cheese butter

SERVES **4**   HANDS-ON TIME: **10 MINUTES**   TOTAL TIME: **24 MINUTES**

1½ pounds fresh green beans, trimmed

2 cups multi-colored grape tomatoes

2 tablespoons olive oil

1½ teaspoons kosher salt

1 teaspoon freshly ground black pepper

2 (12- to 16-ounce) boneless rib-eye steaks (about 1¼ inches thick)

3 tablespoons unsalted butter, softened

1½ tablespoons crumbled blue cheese

½ teaspoon chopped fresh thyme

1 Preheat the broiler, with the oven rack 6 to 8 inches from the heat.

2 Place the green beans and tomatoes on a large baking sheet. Drizzle with the olive oil, and sprinkle with 1 teaspoon of the salt and ½ teaspoon of the pepper; toss well.

3 Broil 5 minutes. Remove the baking sheet from the oven. Sprinkle the remaining ½ teaspoon each salt and pepper on the steaks. Arrange the steaks on the baking sheet in a single layer, moving aside the green beans and tomatoes to make room.

4 Return the baking sheet to the oven; broil the steaks until the desired degree of doneness, 2 to 4 minutes on each side. Remove from the oven; let the steaks rest 5 minutes.

5 Combine the butter, blue cheese, and thyme in a small bowl; stir well. Serve the butter mixture over the steaks.

prep pointer   You can also use hanger steak, New York strip steak, or flank steak.

This is a dinner-party worthy dish that couldn't be easier to prepare. For an extra burst of flavor, stir a few tablespoons of the pan drippings into your sour cream.

ancho chile flank steak AND sweet potato tacos

SERVES **6 TO 8**   HANDS-ON TIME: **18 MINUTES**   TOTAL TIME: **1 HOUR, 55 MINUTES, INCLUDES CHILLING**

1 (2-pound) flank steak
¼ cup fresh lime juice (2 limes)
¼ cup chopped fresh cilantro
½ teaspoon garlic powder
1 tablespoon plus 1 teaspoon ground cumin
1 tablespoon plus 1 teaspoon ancho chile powder
4 teaspoons kosher salt
¼ cup plus 2 tablespoons olive oil
½ pound fresh tomatillos, husks removed
1½ pounds sweet potatoes, peeled and cut into
   ¾-inch pieces
1 large red onion, cut into ½-inch pieces
Flour tortillas, sour cream, fresh cilantro leaves

1 Place the flank steak in a large zip-top plastic freezer bag. Stir together the lime juice, chopped cilantro, and garlic powder, 1 tablespoon of the cumin, 1 tablespoon of the ancho chile powder, and 2 teaspoons of the kosher salt in a small bowl. Whisk in ¼ cup of the olive oil, and pour over the flank steak. Seal the bag, and turn to coat. Chill 1 to 12 hours.

2 Place the oven rack about 6 inches from the heat. Preheat the oven to 450°F.

3 Rinse the tomatillos, and cut into quarters. Stir together the sweet potatoes, red onion, tomatillos, and remaining 1 teaspoon each cumin and ancho chile powder, 2 teaspoons salt, and 2 tablespoons oil in a large bowl. Spread the sweet potato mixture in an even layer on a heavy-duty aluminum foil–lined baking sheet.

4 Bake at 450°F for 20 minutes. Remove from the oven, and move the sweet potato mixture to the outer edges of the baking sheet. Remove the flank steak from the marinade; discard the marinade. Place the flank steak in the center of the baking sheet. Increase the oven temperature to broil.

5 Broil 6 minutes. Turn the steak over, and broil 6 more minutes. (Stir the vegetables if they begin to char.) Remove from the oven, and let stand 5 minutes. Cut the steak across the grain, and drizzle with the pan drippings. Serve with the sweet potato mixture, tortillas, sour cream, and fresh cilantro.

This one-sheet meal is a crowd-pleaser and testament to how four ingredients can come together quickly to form a supremely satisfying dish. We broil the steak over the veggies so the meat juices baste them as they cook.

broiled flat iron steak WITH brussels sprouts AND sweet potatoes

SERVES **4**   HANDS-ON TIME: **15 MINUTES**   TOTAL TIME: **35 MINUTES**

6 ounces fresh Brussels sprouts, trimmed and halved

6 ounces sweet potatoes, peeled, halved lengthwise, and sliced into thin half-moons

2 tablespoons olive oil

1 (1-pound) flat iron steak, trimmed

2 teaspoons chopped fresh thyme

1 teaspoon kosher salt

¾ teaspoon freshly ground black pepper

1 Preheat the broiler, with the oven rack 6 inches from the heat.

2 Place the Brussels sprouts and potatoes on a baking sheet; toss with 1 tablespoon of the oil, and spread in an even layer. Place a wire rack on the baking sheet over the vegetables.

Rub the steak with 1½ teaspoons of the oil, and place on the rack on the baking sheet over the vegetables. Sprinkle the steak with 1 teaspoon of the thyme, ½ teaspoon of the salt, and half of the pepper.

3 Broil 10 minutes, and then turn the steak over; drizzle with the remaining 1½ teaspoons oil, and sprinkle with the remaining thyme, salt, and pepper. Broil until the desired degree of doneness, about 5 minutes.

4 Remove the steak from the baking sheet, and let stand 5 minutes. Cut across the grain into thin slices. Place the vegetables in a bowl; pour in the pan juices, and toss to coat.

When you're craving comfort food, look no further than these easy, cheesy Meatball Calzones. Premade pizza dough is our secret ingredient for cutting down on prep time. Serve the calzones with a fresh salad or with Roasted Beet Hummus (page 221) and crudités.

meatball calzones

SERVES **4**   HANDS-ON TIME: **20 MINUTES**   TOTAL TIME: **1 HOUR, 5 MINUTES**

8 ounces ground beef

½ small onion, finely chopped

2 garlic cloves, minced

1 teaspoon Italian seasoning

⅓ cup fresh breadcrumbs

½ teaspoon table salt

½ teaspoon freshly ground black pepper

½ cup tomato sauce

1 pound pizza dough, thawed if frozen

2 ounces mozzarella, shredded (about ½ cup)

1 large egg

1 tablespoon water

1 Preheat the oven to 400°F. Line a baking sheet with aluminum foil.

2 Mix together the beef, onion, garlic, Italian seasoning, breadcrumbs, salt, and pepper in a bowl until well combined. Shape the mixture into 16 (1-inch) balls and place on the prepared baking sheet. Bake at 400°F for 12 to 15 minutes, turning often. Place the tomato sauce in a large bowl. Toss the meatballs with the sauce and set aside to cool.

3 Reduce the oven temperature to 375°F. Line a baking sheet with foil and lightly coat with cooking spray. Divide the dough into 4 pieces. Roll each piece into a 7- to 8-inch circle. Divide the meatballs among the dough circles, placing them slightly off center and leaving a 1-inch border. Sprinkle each calzone with the mozzarella. Fold the dough over the filling and roll the bottom edge over the top, pressing and crimping together to seal. Beat the egg and water and brush all over the calzones. Make a slit in the top of each calzone to let steam escape. Place the calzones on the prepared baking sheet. Bake at 375°F until golden brown, about 40 minutes. Let rest for 5 minutes before serving.

prep pointer

If you are using the same baking sheet to bake the calzones that you used to bake the meatballs, make sure you cool the baking sheet completely before placing the calzones on it to ensure even browning.

Fans of Greek food will love these meatballs—made with ground lamb, golden raisins, cinnamon, scallions—and their minty yogurt topping. This recipe creates a delicious meal right on a baking sheet. Serve these gyros with Roasted Vegetables (page 132) or raw vegggies with one of our hummus recipes (pages 218-223) to bulk up the meal.

lamb meatball gyros WITH yogurt AND mint

SERVES **4**   HANDS-ON TIME: **25 MINUTES**   TOTAL TIME: **31 MINUTES**

1 pound ground lamb
¼ cup golden raisins, chopped
¼ teaspoon ground cinnamon
1½ teaspoons kosher salt
¼ teaspoon freshly ground black pepper
½ cup fine, dry breadcrumbs
1 large egg, beaten
1 bunch scallions (white and light green parts), sliced
4 pieces flat bread
½ cup plain Greek yogurt
2 tablespoons fresh mint leaves

1 Place an oven rack in the second-highest position. Preheat the broiler.

2 Combine the lamb, raisins, cinnamon, salt, pepper, breadcrumbs, egg, and three-quarters of the scallions in a large bowl.

3 Shape the mixture into golf ball–sized meatballs and place on an aluminum foil–lined baking sheet.

4 Broil, turning once, until cooked through, 6 to 8 minutes.

5 Divide the flat bread among each of 4 plates. Top with the meatballs, yogurt, mint, and remaining scallions.

This new spin on meatloaf couldn't be easier to prepare.

mini meat loaves WITH potatoes, leeks, AND brussels sprouts

SERVES **4**   HANDS-ON TIME: **15 MINUTES**   TOTAL TIME: **1 HOUR**

5 tablespoons olive oil

2 teaspoons chopped garlic (about 2 garlic cloves)

1 teaspoon grated lemon rind plus 2 tablespoons fresh juice

1 teaspoon kosher salt

¾ teaspoon freshly ground black pepper

12 ounces fresh Brussels sprouts, trimmed and halved

1 leek, chopped

8 ounces baby red potatoes (about 7), cut into wedges

8 ounces lean ground beef

8 ounces mild ground pork sausage

¼ cup grated carrot (from 1 carrot)

¼ cup grated yellow onion (from 1 onion)

¼ cup fine, dry breadcrumbs

1 large egg, lightly beaten

¼ cup ketchup

1 teaspoon soy sauce

1 tablespoon chopped fresh flat-leaf parsley

1 Preheat the oven to 400°F.

2 Whisk together the oil, garlic, lemon rind, lemon juice, ½ teaspoon of the kosher salt, and ¼ teaspoon of the pepper in a large bowl.

Add the Brussels sprouts, leek, and red potatoes, and toss to coat. Spread the vegetables on a lightly greased, aluminum foil–lined baking sheet. Bake the vegetables at 400°F for 10 minutes.

3 Meanwhile, combine the beef, sausage, carrot, onion, breadcrumbs, egg, and remaining ½ teaspoon each salt and pepper in a large bowl. Mix gently just until combined. Shape into 4 (2- x 3-inch) loaves. Remove the baking sheet from the oven, push the vegetables to one side, and carefully place the meat loaves on the baking sheet. Return the baking sheet to the oven, and bake until the meat is cooked through and the vegetables are tender, about 35 minutes.

4 Whisk together the ketchup and soy sauce in a small bowl. Spread over the meat loaves. Increase the oven temperature to broil, and broil until the sauce begins to brown, about 2 minutes. Place the meat loaves and vegetables evenly on each of 4 plates. Sprinkle evenly with the parsley.

main dishes

103

Apples, brown sugar, and cinnamon add sweet complexity to this dish.

pork chops WITH roasted apples AND brussels sprouts

SERVES **4**   HANDS-ON TIME: **15 MINUTES**   TOTAL TIME: **40 MINUTES**

1 teaspoon paprika
1 teaspoon chili powder
1 teaspoon garlic salt
⅛ teaspoon ground red pepper
⅛ teaspoon ground cinnamon
3 tablespoons light brown sugar
2 teaspoons finely chopped fresh rosemary
1 teaspoon kosher salt
½ teaspoon freshly ground black pepper
4 (1-inch-thick) bone-in, center-cut pork chops
3 tablespoons plus 2 teaspoons olive oil
3 tablespoons apple cider vinegar
1 Gala apple (8 to 9 ounces), cut into ½-inch wedges
1 pound fresh Brussels sprouts, trimmed and halved
Kosher salt

1 Preheat the oven to 425°F.

2 Stir together the paprika, chili powder, garlic salt, red pepper, cinnamon, 1 tablespoon of the brown sugar, 1 teaspoon of the rosemary, ½ teaspoon of the salt, and ¼ teaspoon of the black pepper in a small bowl. Rub each pork chop with ½ teaspoon of the olive oil; rub both sides of each pork chop with the brown sugar mixture (about 2 teaspoons on each chop).

3 Whisk together the apple cider vinegar and the remaining 2 tablespoons brown sugar, 1 teaspoon rosemary, ½ teaspoon salt, and

¼ teaspoon black pepper in a small bowl; slowly whisk in the remaining 3 tablespoons olive oil until blended. Place the apples, Brussels sprouts, and ¼ cup of the vinegar mixture in a large bowl; toss to coat.

4 Place the pork chops in the center of a heavy-duty aluminum foil–lined baking sheet lightly greased with cooking spray; place the apple mixture around the pork chops.

5 Bake at 425°F for 12 minutes; turn the pork chops over, and bake until a meat thermometer inserted in the thickest portion registers 140°F, 10 to 14 more minutes. Transfer the pork chops to a serving platter, and cover with foil to keep warm. Stir the apple mixture on the baking sheet, and spread into an even layer.

6 Increase the oven temperature to broil, and broil the apple mixture 3 to 4 minutes or until browned and slightly charred. Transfer the apple mixture to a medium bowl. Toss together the apple mixture and the remaining vinegar mixture. Season with the kosher salt, and serve with the pork chops.

This dish is perfect for a busy weeknight. Marinate the chops in the morning before work. When you get home, bake the veggies and chops, and you'll have dinner on the table in less than an hour.

greek pork chops WITH squash AND potatoes

SERVES **4**   HANDS-ON TIME: **20 MINUTES**   TOTAL TIME: **1 HOUR, 53 MINUTES, INCLUDES CHILLING**

4 (1-inch-thick) frenched pork loin chops
½ cup fresh lemon juice
4 tablespoons olive oil
3 garlic cloves, minced
3 tablespoons chopped fresh oregano
1 teaspoon freshly ground black pepper
3 teaspoons kosher salt
2 medium-sized yellow squash, sliced ½-inch thick
1 large zucchini, sliced ½-inch thick
½ pound baby red potatoes (about 7), quartered

1 Place the pork chops in a large zip-top plastic freezer bag or a baking dish. Whisk together the lemon juice, oil, garlic, oregano, pepper, and 2½ teaspoons of the salt; reserve 2 tablespoons of the marinade. Pour the remaining marinade into the freezer bag over the pork, and seal. Chill 1 to 8 hours.

2 Preheat the oven to 425°F.

3 Combine the squash, zucchini, potatoes, and reserved marinade in a large bowl; toss to coat. Spread the squash mixture in an even layer on a heavy-duty aluminum foil–lined baking sheet.

4 Remove the pork from the marinade; discard the marinade. Pat dry with paper towels, and place on top of the squash mixture.

5 Bake at 425°F for 25 minutes. Increase the temperature to broil, and broil until a meat thermometer inserted into the thickest portion registers 140°F, about 5 minutes. Transfer the pork to a serving platter, and cover with foil. Return the baking sheet to the oven, and broil the squash mixture until slightly charred, 3 to 4 minutes. Transfer the squash mixture to a serving bowl; toss with the remaining ½ teaspoon salt, and serve with the pork.

You'll love this delicious, company-worthy pork chop dinner! The chops roast along with beets, which combine with hearty kale and a tangy thyme-honey-mustard dressing to make a colorful winter salad. (Also pictured on page 44)

broiled pork chops WITH beets AND kale

SERVES **4**   HANDS-ON TIME: **10 MINUTES**   TOTAL TIME: **40 MINUTES**

1 pound baby beets, peeled and halved

2 teaspoons grated garlic (about 3 garlic cloves)

3 tablespoons olive oil

1 teaspoon kosher salt

¾ teaspoon freshly ground black pepper

4 (12-ounce) bone-in pork loin chops

¼ cup sour cream

1 tablespoon Dijon mustard

1 tablespoon honey

1 tablespoon chopped fresh thyme

3 cups finely shredded curly kale (stems removed)

1 Preheat the broiler, with the oven rack about 10 inches from the heat.

2 Toss together the beets, grated garlic, 1 tablespoon of the oil, and ¼ teaspoon each of the salt and pepper. Place on a large aluminum foil–lined baking sheet lightly greased with cooking spray. Broil for 10 minutes.

3 Meanwhile, rub the pork chops with 1 tablespoon of the olive oil, and sprinkle with ½ teaspoon of the salt and ¼ teaspoon of the pepper. Remove the beets from the oven, and nestle the pork chops into the beets. Return the baking sheet to the oven. Broil until the pork is just cooked through and the beets are tender, about 15 minutes.

4 Whisk together the sour cream, mustard, honey, 1 teaspoon of the thyme, the remaining ¼ teaspoon each of the salt and pepper, and the remaining 1 tablespoon oil in a small bowl. Transfer the cooked beets to a large bowl; add the shredded kale and 2 tablespoons of the sour cream mixture, and toss to coat. Cover with plastic wrap, and let stand 5 minutes. Serve the pork chops over the vegetable mixture. Sprinkle with the remaining 2 teaspoons thyme, and serve with the remaining sour cream mixture.

prep pointer

You can make the dressing 1 day before, and store it covered in the refrigerator.

This recipe is the perfect solution for anyone who craves steamed buns but doesn't own a steamer. Here, we create a pseudo-steamer using the ever-versatile sheet pan: Simply place a wire rack (for the buns to sit on) in a sheet pan filled with a shallow layer of water, and tent the buns loosely with foil. While you steam the buns, you'll use another sheet pan to simultaneously cook the deliciously crispy pulled pork that you'll fill the buns with.

carnitas bao buns

SERVES **2**   HANDS-ON TIME: **15 MINUTES**   TOTAL TIME: **27 MINUTES**

½ cup water
8 (3½-inch) frozen bao buns
1 pound pulled pork
¼ cup gochujang (such as Bibigo)
3 tablespoons Kewpie mayonnaise
1½ tablespoons ponzu sauce (such as Kikkoman)
1½ tablespoons unseasoned rice vinegar
1 cup sliced English cucumber
½ cup matchstick carrots
¼ cup fried shallots (such as Maesri)
¼ cup packed fresh cilantro leaves
Lime wedges

1 Preheat the oven to 475°F with 1 rack in the top third of the oven and 1 rack in the bottom third of the oven. Place a wire rack on a baking sheet; lightly grease the rack. Coat a large piece of aluminum foil with cooking spray. Pour the water into the baking sheet. Place the buns on the rack, and tent with the prepared foil, cooking spray side down, sealing tightly at the edges.

2 Lightly grease an aluminum foil–lined baking sheet. Spread the pork in an even layer on the prepared baking sheet. Place the pork on the top oven rack and the buns on the bottom rack; bake 10 minutes. Increase the heat to broil, and broil until the pork begins to crisp, 2 to 4 minutes.

3 Stir together the gochujang, mayonnaise, ponzu, and rice vinegar. Toss the crispy pork in the gochujang mixture, and divide evenly among the buns. Top evenly with the cucumber, carrots, shallots, and cilantro. Serve with the lime wedges.

flavor note

You can find frozen bao buns at your local Asian market—and you can also pick up gochujang, ponzu sauce, and Kewpie mayo there as well. We prefer Kewpie in this recipe, as it is a bit sweeter than typical mayonnaise. If you want to cut back on the heat, reduce the gochujang by 1 tablespoon.

If you're lucky enough to have leftovers, wrap the hoagies in foil, and reheat in a 350°F oven for 15 minutes.

bratwurst WITH peppers AND onions

SERVES **6**   HANDS-ON TIME: **15 MINUTES**   TOTAL TIME: **1 HOUR**

2 large red bell peppers, cut into strips
1 large yellow bell pepper, cut into strips
2 large sweet onions, cut into strips
1 tablespoon olive oil
1 teaspoon kosher salt
¼ teaspoon freshly ground black pepper
6 fresh bratwurst sausages (about 1½ pounds)
6 hoagie rolls, lightly toasted and split

1 Preheat the oven to 375°F.

2 Toss together the bell peppers, onions, olive oil, salt, and pepper in a large bowl; spread the mixture in an even layer on a heavy-duty aluminum foil–lined baking sheet lightly greased with cooking spray.

3 Pierce each sausage 6 times with a wooden pick. Place the sausages 3 to 4 inches apart on top of the pepper mixture.

4 Bake at 375°F for 40 minutes; increase the oven temperature to broil. Broil until the sausages are browned, 6 to 8 minutes, turning the sausages halfway through.

5 Place 1 sausage in each roll, and top with the desired amount of pepper mixture.

flavor note

Serve these hoagies with a spicy mustard topping. The heat will pair well with the sweet peppers and onions.

Serving brunch to a large group has never been so easy or delicious. Feel free to top off this large, savory pancake with a few frizzled fried eggs and serve with mimosas.

giant bacon–green chile dutch baby

SERVES **8**　HANDS-ON TIME: **15 MINUTES**　TOTAL TIME: **51 MINUTES**

1 pound thick-cut bacon slices, chopped

1½ cups whole milk

6 large eggs

1½ cups all-purpose flour (about 6½ ounces)

3 tablespoons granulated sugar

¾ teaspoon kosher salt, divided

1 (4-ounce) can chopped green chiles, drained

1 tablespoon extra-virgin olive oil

2 teaspoons fresh lime juice

¼ teaspoon ancho chile powder

¼ teaspoon honey

1 cup packed arugula

½ cup cherry tomatoes, halved

½ cup fresh corn kernels

1½ ounces Cotija cheese, crumbled (about ⅓ cup)

1 Preheat the oven to 425°F.

2 Scatter the bacon evenly on a half-sized baking sheet. Bake at 425°F until the bacon begins to crisp and the fat has rendered, 16 to 18 minutes.

3 Process the milk and eggs in a blender until smooth, about 30 seconds. Stir together the flour, sugar, and ¼ teaspoon of the salt in a medium bowl. Add the flour mixture to the milk mixture; process until smooth, about 30 seconds. Pour the batter evenly over the bacon, and sprinkle evenly with the green chiles. Bake at 425°F until golden brown and puffy, about 20 minutes.

4 Whisk together the oil, lime juice, chile powder, honey, and remaining ½ teaspoon salt in a large bowl. Add the arugula, tomatoes, and corn; toss to coat. Top the Dutch baby evenly with arugula mixture; sprinkle evenly with cheese. Serve immediately.

prep pointer　Use your heaviest, flat baking sheet for this recipe, to minimize any risk of warping.

side dishes

Roasted to perfection, this is a quick and supereasy side for any meal.

roasted brussels sprouts

SERVES **4**   HANDS-ON TIME: **5 MINUTES**   TOTAL TIME: **22 MINUTES**

1 pound Brussels sprouts, trimmed and halved
1½ tablespoons olive oil
½ teaspoon freshly ground black pepper
¼ teaspoon table salt

1 Preheat the oven to 450°F.

2 Place the Brussels sprouts on a baking sheet coated with cooking spray. Drizzle with the oil; toss to coat. Sprinkle with the pepper and salt. Bake at 450°F until tender (do not stir), 17 minutes.

prep pointer

This is a solid base recipe for a sundry of vegetables. Swap the Brussels sprouts for diced sweet potatoes, radishes, squash, turnips, beets, or other veggies—or create a mixture using some or all—and roast until tender, anywhere from 20 to 45 minutes depending on how much and what type of vegetables you use. For low-moisture vegetables like squash and root vegetables, use lower heat and roast for longer.

Simple and delicious cooking doesn't get any easier than this. Toss all the ingredients on the baking sheet, and let them bake in the oven for about half an hour. Come back to crisp-tender veggie perfection. (Pictured on page 116)

roasted green beans

SERVES **4**   HANDS-ON TIME: **10 MINUTES**   TOTAL TIME: **35 MINUTES**

1 tablespoon olive oil

¼ teaspoon table salt

¼ teaspoon freshly ground black pepper

10 ounces French green beans, trimmed

2 garlic cloves, thinly sliced

1 Preheat the oven to 425°F.

2 Combine all the ingredients on a jelly-roll pan lightly coated with cooking spray; toss to coat.

3 Place the pan on the bottom rack in the oven. Bake at 425°F for 25 minutes, stirring once.

prep pointer

Add 1 pound of fingerling potatoes, halved lengthwise, to amp up the dish. Not a fan of green beans? Use asparagus or sugar snap peas instead. They only need about 15 minutes of roasting time; be sure to monitor their cooking so they don't char.

This is a dinner guests–worthy side dish that's simple to make and looks pretty on a serving platter. Be sure to sprinkle on the blue cheese right away, so it melts slightly onto the asparagus spears.

balsamic–blue cheese asparagus

SERVES **4**   HANDS-ON TIME: **5 MINUTES**   TOTAL TIME: **13 MINUTES**

1 pound fresh asparagus
1 tablespoon balsamic vinegar
2 teaspoons olive oil
1 large garlic clove, minced
2 tablespoons blue cheese, crumbled
¼ teaspoon table salt
¼ teaspoon freshly ground black pepper

1 Preheat the oven to 400°F.

2 Snap off the tough ends of the asparagus; discard the ends. Arrange the asparagus in a single layer on a jelly-roll pan. Combine the vinegar, oil, and garlic; drizzle over the asparagus. Bake at 400°F for 8 to 12 minutes.

3 Place the asparagus on a platter; sprinkle with the cheese, salt, and pepper.

flavor note

Parmesan or shredded mozzarella make pleasing substitutions if a guest dislikes the sharp, salty, and pungent blue cheese.

This recipe flourishes as a show-stopping side dish that gets added flavor from lemon rind, Parmesan cheese, and panko.

broiled artichoke hearts WITH lemon crumbs

SERVES **4**   HANDS-ON TIME: **5 MINUTES**   TOTAL TIME: **10 MINUTES**

½ cup panko (Japanese breadcrumbs)

1 tablespoon grated Parmesan cheese

2 teaspoons butter, melted

1 teaspoon grated lemon rind

½ teaspoon freshly ground black pepper

2 (9-ounce) packages frozen artichoke hearts, thawed

1½ teaspoons olive oil

⅛ teaspoon kosher salt

1 Preheat the broiler.

2 Combine the panko, Parmesan cheese, melted butter, lemon rind, and pepper in a bowl.

3 Toss the thawed artichoke hearts with the olive oil and salt on a baking sheet. Top with the panko mixture. Broil 6 inches from the heat until slightly browned, 5 to 6 minutes.

prep pointer

In broiling, food is cooked by direct heat coming from the oven's heat source above; whereas in baking, the food is surrounded by hot air. Broiling temperature is typically between 500° and 550°F.

Cauliflower isn't usually a favorite among kids, but they will adore this oven-roasted version, which caramelizes the vegetable's natural sugars, leaving it incredibly sweet.

roasted cauliflower WITH sage

SERVES **6**   HANDS-ON TIME: **7 MINUTES**   TOTAL TIME: **19 MINUTES**

1 (1¾-pound) head cauliflower, trimmed and cut into
   1½-inch florets
1 tablespoon olive oil
½ teaspoon freshly ground black pepper
¼ teaspoon table salt
2 tablespoons fresh sage leaves
2 teaspoons peeled lemon rind strips

1 Preheat the oven to 500°F.

2 Place a large baking sheet in the oven. Heat 5 minutes.

3 While the baking sheet heats, place the cauliflower in a large bowl. Drizzle the cauliflower with the oil; toss until coated. Sprinkle with the pepper and salt; toss well. Carefully remove the preheated baking sheet from the oven. Spread the cauliflower in a single layer on the hot baking sheet.

4 Bake at 500°F until browned and tender, about 12 minutes. Transfer the cauliflower to a bowl. Add the sage and lemon rind; toss well. Serve immediately.

You can easily double or triple this recipe. Be sure to use the largest baking sheet you have or use two smaller sheets—whatever keeps the carrots from being stacked. You may need to increase the bake time. The carrots will be done when they are crisp-tender. (Also pictured on page 116)

chile AND **lime roasted carrots**

SERVES **2**   HANDS-ON TIME: **5 MINUTES**   TOTAL TIME: **20 MINUTES**

1 teaspoon olive oil
¼ teaspoon crushed red pepper
8 ounces baby carrots with tops
⅛ teaspoon kosher salt
Lime wedges

1 Preheat the oven to 500°F.

2 Combine the oil, pepper, and carrots on a baking sheet; toss to coat. Bake at 500°F for 15 minutes, stirring after 10 minutes. Sprinkle with the salt. Serve with the lime wedges.

flavor note

Turn up the heat by adding seeded and finely chopped jalapeño chile.

These breaded and broiled tomatoes burst with warm juiciness at every bite. Eat them with a simple roasted chicken or fish such as Roasted Salmon with Thyme and Honey-Mustard Glaze (page 56).

herbed breadcrumb tomatoes

SERVES **2**　HANDS-ON TIME: **3 MINUTES**　TOTAL TIME: **30 MINUTES**

¼ cup whole-wheat panko (Japanese breadcrumbs)

2 teaspoons olive oil

1½ teaspoons chopped fresh thyme

1½ teaspoons chopped fresh flat-leaf parsley

¼ teaspoon freshly ground black pepper

⅛ teaspoon kosher salt

2 tomatoes, halved horizontally (8 ounces)

Cooking spray

1 Preheat the oven to 425°F.

2 Combine the first 6 ingredients in a small bowl. Place the tomato halves, cut sides up, on an aluminum foil–lined baking sheet coated with cooking spray. Top the tomatoes with the panko mixture; coat with the cooking spray. Bake at 425°F for 25 minutes. Turn the broiler to high (do not remove the baking sheet from the oven). Broil until the topping is browned, 2 minutes.

prep pointer

Coating foods—such as the panko-topped tomatoes in this recipe—with cooking spray helps ensure even cooking and makes them extra crispy.

This elevated take on the humble carrot and parsnip is worthy of a holiday dinner. You can swap Gorgonzola for the feta and dried cranberries or raisins for the cherries, depending on what you have.

balsamic-roasted carrots AND parsnips

SERVES **8 TO 10**   HANDS-ON TIME: **20 MINUTES**   TOTAL TIME: **1 HOUR**

4 ounces feta cheese, crumbled (about 1 cup)
½ cup chopped dried sweet cherries
¼ cup chopped fresh flat-leaf parsley
1 teaspoon grated lemon rind
½ teaspoon crushed red pepper
4 tablespoons olive oil
1½ pounds carrots, peeled and sliced into thin strips
1½ pounds parsnips, peeled and sliced into thin strips
2 tablespoons light brown sugar
3 tablespoons balsamic vinegar
½ teaspoon table salt
½ teaspoon freshly ground black pepper

1 Preheat the oven to 400°F.

2 Toss together the feta, cherries, parsley, rind, red pepper, and 1 tablespoon of the olive oil in a small bowl.

3 Cut the carrots and parsnips lengthwise into long, thin strips.

4 Whisk together the brown sugar, balsamic vinegar, and remaining 3 tablespoons olive oil in a large bowl. Toss with the carrots and parsnips, and place on a lightly greased jelly-roll pan. Sprinkle with the salt and pepper.

5 Bake at 400°F until the vegetables are tender and browned, stirring every 15 minutes, 40 to 45 minutes. Transfer to a serving platter, and gently toss with the feta cheese mixture.

If you're not familiar with parsnips, they look like white carrots and have a decidedly sweet, earthy flavor. Avoid larger parsnips, which tend to have tough, woody cores.

roasted parsnips WITH lemon AND herbs

SERVES **4**   HANDS-ON TIME: **5 MINUTES**   TOTAL TIME: **15 MINUTES**

1 pound parsnips, peeled and sliced into thin strips
2 tablespoons fresh lemon juice
1 tablespoon extra-virgin olive oil
½ teaspoon freshly ground black pepper
¼ teaspoon kosher salt
¼ cup chopped fresh flat-leaf parsley
1 tablespoon chopped fresh dill
Lemon wedges

1 Preheat the oven to 500°F. Place a baking sheet in the oven (do not remove the baking sheet from the oven).

2 Combine the parsnips, juice, oil, pepper, and salt in a bowl. Carefully remove the baking sheet from the oven. Arrange the vegetable mixture in a single layer on the baking sheet. Bake at 500°F until tender, about 10 minutes. Toss with the parsley and dill. Serve with the lemon wedges.

flavor note

For a variation, follow the main recipe through Step 1. Toss together 1 pound parsnips, peeled and sliced into thin strips; 1½ tablespoons chopped walnuts; 1 tablespoon chopped fresh thyme; 2 tablespoons maple syrup; ¼ teaspoon kosher salt; and ¼ teaspoon freshly ground black pepper. Arrange in 1 layer on the preheated baking sheet; bake until tender, about 10 minutes. Toss with ½ teaspoon sherry vinegar.

During the last 5 minutes of cooking time, crack an egg (or multiple) over the roasting veggies to turn this hearty side into a meal.

roasted vegetables

SERVES **10**   HANDS-ON TIME: **15 MINUTES**   TOTAL TIME: **50 MINUTES**

3 tablespoons olive oil

2 tablespoons whole-grain mustard

1 tablespoon chopped fresh thyme

1 tablespoon apple cider vinegar

¾ teaspoon kosher salt

½ teaspoon freshly ground black pepper

1 pound peeled cubed butternut squash (about 3 cups)

1 pound parsnips, peeled and cut into 1-inch pieces (about 2¼ cups)

1 pound Brussels sprouts, trimmed and halved

8 ounces small Yukon Gold potatoes, halved

1 Preheat the oven to 450°F.

2 Combine the oil, mustard, thyme, 2 teaspoons of the vinegar, salt, and pepper in a bowl, stirring with a whisk. Combine the butternut squash, parsnips, Brussels sprouts, and potatoes in a large bowl. Add the mustard mixture to the squash mixture; toss to coat.

3 Spread the vegetable mixture in a single layer on an aluminum foil–lined baking sheet coated with cooking spray. Bake at 450°F until browned and tender, stirring gently with a spatula after 25 minutes, 35 minutes. Remove the baking sheet from the oven. Drizzle with the remaining 1 teaspoon vinegar; toss.

flavor note

For a variation, combine 3 tablespoons olive oil, 1 tablespoon maple syrup, 1 tablespoon fresh orange juice, 2 teaspoons chopped fresh tarragon, 1 teaspoon kosher salt, and ½ teaspoon freshly ground black pepper in a bowl, stirring with a whisk. Combine the butternut squash, parsnips, Brussels sprouts, and potatoes from the above recipe in a large bowl. Add the orange juice mixture to the vegetables; toss to coat. Bake as directed in Step 3 of the above recipe. Remove the baking sheet from the oven; sprinkle the vegetables with 1 teaspoon orange rind strips, 1 tablespoon fresh orange juice, and 1 teaspoon chopped fresh tarragon; toss.

The broiler brings alive the flavors of late-fall corn and peppers so they taste as good as at summer's peak. To help control the broiler's heat, move foods closer to or farther away from the element—not just up or down the oven racks but also toward or away from the sides.

mexican broiled corn salad

SERVES **8**   HANDS-ON TIME: **45 MINUTES**   TOTAL TIME: **1 HOUR, 23 MINUTES**

4 ears fresh corn, shucked
1 medium onion, cut into ½-inch-thick slices
2 red bell peppers
1 tablespoon chopped fresh oregano
½ teaspoon kosher salt
1 cup grape tomatoes, halved
1 cup thinly sliced radishes
3½ tablespoons extra-virgin olive oil
2 tablespoons chopped fresh cilantro
5 tablespoons hulled pepitas (pumpkin seeds), toasted
1 tablespoon chopped jalapeño chile
2 tablespoons fresh lime juice
1 tablespoon honey
1 teaspoon ground ancho chile powder
¼ teaspoon ground cumin
2 garlic cloves, crushed
2½ ounces cotija cheese, crumbled (about ⅔ cup)

1 Preheat the broiler to high.

2 Place the corn and onion on an aluminum foil-lined baking sheet lightly coated with cooking spray. Broil 4 inches from the heat 15 minutes, turning occasionally. Cut the bell peppers in half lengthwise; discard the seeds and membranes. Place the bell pepper halves, skin sides up, on the baking sheet with the corn and onion. Broil until all the vegetables are charred in spots, turning the corn and onion occasionally (do not turn the bell peppers), 13 more minutes. Place the bell peppers in a paper bag. Fold to close tightly; let stand 10 minutes. Peel and coarsely chop the peppers. Cut the kernels from the ears of the corn. Coarsely chop the onion. Place the bell peppers, corn, onion, oregano, and ⅛ teaspoon of the salt in a medium bowl; toss gently.

3 Combine ⅛ teaspoon of the salt, tomatoes, radishes, 1½ teaspoons of the oil, and cilantro in a medium bowl; toss to coat.

4 Place 2 tablespoons of the pumpkin seeds in a mini food processor; process until finely ground. Add the remaining ¼ teaspoon salt, remaining 3 tablespoons oil, jalapeño, lime juice, honey, chile powder, cumin and garlic; process until smooth.

5 Place ½ cup of the corn mixture in each of 8 shallow bowls, and top each serving with about 2 tablespoons of the tomato mixture, 1 tablespoon of the dressing, about 1½ tablespoons of the cheese, and about 1 teaspoon of the remaining pumpkin seeds.

Instead of buying prediced butternut squash, you can dice your own. To make the dicing easier, place the squash in the microwave and heat it at HIGH for about 2 minutes before peeling and chopping.

roasted butternut squash WITH pecans AND sage

SERVES **4**   HANDS-ON TIME: **5 MINUTES**   TOTAL TIME: **20 MINUTES**

2 (11-ounce) containers peeled diced fresh butternut squash
Cooking spray
¼ teaspoon kosher salt
¼ teaspoon freshly ground black pepper
1½ tablespoons butter, melted
2 tablespoons chopped pecans, toasted
1 tablespoon finely chopped fresh sage

1 Preheat the oven to 425°F.

2 Arrange the butternut squash in a single layer on a baking sheet; coat with cooking spray. Sprinkle evenly with the salt and pepper. Bake at 425°F until browned, stirring halfway through cooking, 15 minutes.

3 Place the butter in a large bowl. Stir in the squash, pecans, and sage; toss to combine.

flavor note

For a variation, follow the main recipe through Step 2. Combine 1 tablespoon fresh lime juice, 1 tablespoon canola oil, 1 teaspoon rice vinegar, and a dash of sugar in a small bowl, stirring with a whisk. Combine the squash, ¼ cup chopped fresh cilantro, ¼ cup toasted unsweetened coconut flakes, and 1 seeded sliced red chile in a large bowl; toss gently to combine. Drizzle the juice mixture over the squash mixture; toss to coat.

If you only have one baking sheet, it's better to save half the seasoned acorn squash and cook it on the same baking sheet after the first batch is finished rather than to overcrowd the pan. Overcrowding can lead to limp or soggy food, as heat and moisture get trapped inside the layers.

chili-roasted acorn squash

SERVES **6**   HANDS-ON TIME: **10 MINUTES**   TOTAL TIME: **45 MINUTES**

2 acorn squash, scrubbed

3 tablespoons olive oil

2 teaspoons chili powder

1 teaspoon ground cumin

½ teaspoon paprika

½ teaspoon table salt, plus more for seasoning (optional)

¼ teaspoon freshly ground black pepper, plus more for seasoning (optional)

1 Preheat the oven to 400°F.

2 Cut each squash in half lengthwise and remove the seeds. Trim and discard the ends; cut each half crosswise into slices that are about 1 inch thick.

3 Place the slices in a large bowl; add the oil, chili powder, cumin, paprika, ½ teaspoon salt, and ¼ teaspoon pepper. Toss to coat. Arrange the slices flat on 2 large baking sheets. Bake at 400°F until lightly browned and tender, turning once, 35 to 40 minutes. Season with additional salt and pepper, if desired.

This is a smart way to use up Brussels sprouts. Pair this recipe with an entrée such as Lamb Meatball Gyros with Yogurt and Mint (page 101).

roasted sweet potatoes, onions, AND brussels sprouts

SERVES **6**   HANDS-ON TIME: **15 MINUTES**   TOTAL TIME: **50 MINUTES**

1 pound sweet potatoes, peeled and cut into 1-inch pieces

1 pound Brussels sprouts, trimmed and halved

1 (14.4-ounce) bag frozen pearl onions, thawed, patted dry

3 garlic cloves, minced

2 teaspoons chopped fresh thyme

2 teaspoons chopped fresh rosemary

1 teaspoon table salt

½ teaspoon freshly ground black pepper

3 tablespoons olive oil

1 Preheat the oven to 400°F.

2 Lightly coat a baking sheet with cooking spray. Combine all the ingredients in a bowl; toss. Spread on the baking sheet in a single layer. Bake at 400°F until tender, 35 to 40 minutes, stirring twice.

prep pointer

If you don't have pearl onions, you can substitute with a diced white or yellow onion.

A quick two-step process of microwave steaming and then roasting creates golden-brown sweet potato wedges for a versatile side dish or even a snack. You can also use the yogurt sauce as a creamy spread or dipper for pita wedges or grilled chicken or lamb.

roasted sweet potato wedges WITH yogurt dipping sauce

SERVES **4**   HANDS-ON TIME: **15 MINUTES**   TOTAL TIME: **38 MINUTES**

3 medium-sized sweet potatoes (about 2 pounds), each halved lengthwise
¼ cup water
1 tablespoon canola oil
¼ teaspoon table salt
¼ teaspoon freshly ground black pepper
¼ cup plain yogurt
2 teaspoons honey
Dash of vanilla extract

1 Preheat the oven to 450°F. Place a large baking sheet in the oven (do not remove the baking sheet from the oven).

2 Place the potatoes and water in a medium microwave-safe bowl. Cover with plastic wrap; pierce with the tip of a knife to vent. Microwave at HIGH for 5 minutes. Drain the water.

3 Cut each potato half lengthwise into 4 wedges.

4 Add the oil to the potatoes; toss to coat.

5 Carefully remove the preheated baking sheet from the oven; coat with cooking spray. Arrange the potatoes in a single layer on the baking sheet; sprinkle with the salt and pepper. Bake at 450°F until browned and tender, 18 minutes.

6 Combine the yogurt, honey, and vanilla, stirring well; serve the sauce with the potatoes.

flavor note

If you're not a fan of yogurt sauce, omit it and instead sprinkle the potatoes with ¼ cup shredded Cheddar or Monterey Jack cheese.

Who doesn't love hot, savory fries? Serve them with a bright salad and Soy Nut–Crusted Catfish (page 66) for a simple and mouthwatering weeknight supper.

oven fries

SERVES **4**   HANDS-ON TIME: **5 MINUTES**   TOTAL TIME: **1 HOUR**

2 large baking potatoes (1¾ pounds), cut lengthwise into ½-inch-thick sticks

¼ cup olive oil

1 teaspoon table salt

½ teaspoon freshly ground black pepper

¾ ounce Parmesan cheese, shaved (about ¼ cup)

1 tablespoon chopped fresh parsley

1 Preheat the oven to 425°F. Place a large baking sheet in the oven for 5 minutes.

2 Toss together the potatoes, olive oil, salt, and black pepper in a large bowl. Carefully remove the preheated baking sheet from the oven. Arrange the potatoes in a single layer on the hot baking sheet. Bake at 425°F until browned and crisp, stirring occasionally, 50 minutes. Toss with the Parmesan and parsley.

prep pointer

Add any fresh herbs you have on hand or sprinkle with a little ground red pepper for some heat — your personal taste preference is the limit.

You don't need a wok for perfectly cooked fried rice. Simply preheat a baking sheet, add oil, and use day-old or microwavable rice. Make sure the rice kernels are separate so that they are evenly toasted and won't glob together. Serve this dish along with mongolian beef, orange chicken, crab rangoons, or spring rolls.

fried rice

SERVES **4**   HANDS-ON TIME: **15 MINUTES**   TOTAL TIME: **25 MINUTES**

⅓ cup mayonnaise

1 tablespoon Sriracha chili sauce

1 tablespoon water

1 tablespoon canola oil

2 (8.8-ounce) pouches microwavable rice
  (such as Uncle Ben's Ready Rice Original)

1 cup frozen peas and carrots blend, thawed

¼ cup chopped scallions (from about 2 scallions)

2 teaspoons chopped garlic (about 2 garlic cloves)

1 tablespoon soy sauce

1 teaspoon toasted sesame oil

5 large eggs

1 Stir together the mayonnaise, Sriracha, and water in a small bowl. Set aside.

2 Preheat the broiler with the oven rack in the center of the oven. Place a baking sheet in the hot oven for 5 minutes. Carefully remove hte preheated baking sheet from the oven. Add the oil and rice to the baking sheet, and carefully stir to coat the rice, breaking up any clumps. Spread the rice into an even layer. Broil, stirring every 3 to 4 minutes, until the rice is light golden brown, 10 to 12 minutes. Add the peas and carrots, scallions, garlic, soy sauce, and sesame oil; toss to coat. Spread the rice mixture in an even layer and, using the back of a spoon, press to form 5 indentations in the rice mixture. Crack the eggs into the indentations; broil until the eggs are set, about 4 minutes. Drizzle with the Sriracha mayonnaise.

flavor note

Top fried rice with rich, runny egg yolk and creamy Sriracha mayo for added texture and flavor.

Creamy loaded potatoes topped with rich Gouda and crumbled bacon is a dinner winner every time. This is a fantastic way to use leftover cooked bacon—also, check out the Prep Pointer for cooking bacon in the oven on page 29. (Pictured on page 117)

loaded twice-baked potatoes

SERVES **4**   HANDS-ON TIME: **9 MINUTES**   TOTAL TIME: **1 HOUR, 16 MINUTES**

2 (8-ounce) baking potatoes
¼ cup plain yogurt
¼ cup milk
2 ounces smoked Gouda cheese, shredded
    (about ½ cup)
½ teaspoon freshly ground black pepper
¼ teaspoon table salt
2 center-cut bacon slices, cooked and crumbled
Sliced green onions (optional)

1 Preheat the oven to 400°F.

2 Pierce the potatoes several times with a fork. Bake at 400°F until tender, 1 hour. Cool slightly. Cut each potato in half lengthwise; scoop out the pulp into a medium bowl, leaving a ¼-inch-thick shell. Add the yogurt and milk to the potato pulp; mash. Stir in 1 ounce of the Gouda and the pepper and salt.

3 Spoon the potato mixture into the potato shells. Place on a baking sheet. Bake at 400°F until thoroughly heated, 5 minutes. Sprinkle with the remaining 1 ounce Gouda.

4 Increase the oven temperature to broil.

5 Broil until the cheese melts, 2 to 3 minutes. Sprinkle evenly with the bacon and, if desired, the green onions.

This gorgeous and hearty salad is brimming with the flavors of fall with ingredients such as pumpkin seeds, Brussels sprouts, cranberries, and dark, leafy greens. Baby kale, which is much more tender and easier to eat uncooked, makes the perfect green to use for a salad like this.

roasted autumn veggie salad
WITH baby kale

SERVES 6   HANDS-ON TIME: **18 MINUTES**   TOTAL TIME: **46 MINUTES**

1½ pounds butternut squash, cut into ¾-inch cubes

1 pound Brussels sprouts, trimmed and halved lengthwise

1 medium-sized red onion, cut into 8 wedges

½ cup plus 1 teaspoon extra-virgin olive oil

4 tablespoons maple syrup

4 thyme sprigs

2 sage sprigs

1¼ teaspoons kosher salt

1 teaspoon freshly ground black pepper

½ cup roasted salted pepitas (pumpkin seeds)

⅛ teaspoon ground red pepper

1 tablespoon whole-grain Dijon mustard

1 tablespoon fresh lemon juice

4 ounces baby kale

¼ cup dried cranberries

4 ounces goat cheese, crumbled (about 1 cup)

Fresh thyme and sage leaves (optional)

1 Preheat the oven to 450°F. Place 2 baking sheets in the oven to preheat.

2 Combine the squash, Brussels sprouts, onion, ¼ cup of the oil, 2 tablespoons of the syrup, thyme, and sage in a large bowl; toss to coat.

Carefully remove the preheated baking sheets from the oven. Coat with cooking spray. Divide the vegetables evenly between the baking sheets. Sprinkle with ¾ teaspoon each of the salt and pepper. Bake at 450°F until browned and tender (do not stir), 20 to 25 minutes. Remove from the oven.

3 Combine 1 teaspoon of the olive oil, pumpkin seeds, and red pepper in a small bowl. Place on a baking sheet and bake at 450°F until lightly toasted, 8 to 10 minutes. Set aside and cool.

4 Combine the remaining ¼ cup oil, 2 tablespoons syrup, ½ teaspoon salt, ¼ teaspoon black pepper, mustard, and lemon juice in a small bowl, stirring with a whisk. Combine 1 tablespoon of the oil mixture and the kale in a large bowl; toss to coat. Add the squash mixture; toss gently to combine. Place the greens mixture on a platter. Drizzle with the remaining dressing; sprinkle with the cranberries and goat cheese and top with the toasted pepitas. Garnish with the thyme and sage, if desired.

Potato salad gets gussied up with a French accent, thanks to Dijon mustard, crème fraîche (a cultured cream with a high content of butterfat), and Champagne vinegar (you can substitute white wine vinegar). This pairs nicely with Rib-Eyes with Veggies and Blue Cheese Butter (page 94).

roasted red bliss potato salad

SERVES **9**   HANDS-ON TIME: **9 MINUTES**   TOTAL TIME: **39 MINUTES**

2 pounds small Red Bliss potatoes, quartered

2 tablespoons olive oil

⅓ cup crème fraîche

3 tablespoons Champagne vinegar or white wine vinegar

2 tablespoons minced shallots

1 teaspoon fresh lemon juice

1 teaspoon Dijon mustard

½ teaspoon table salt

¼ teaspoon freshly ground black pepper

2 tablespoons chopped fresh chives

1 tablespoon chopped fresh parsley

1 Preheat the oven to 400°F.

2 Toss together the potatoes and oil; place in a single layer on a jelly-roll pan. Bake at 400°F until lightly browned, 30 to 35 minutes.

3 Meanwhile, whisk together the crème fraîche, vinegar, shallots, lemon juice, Dijon mustard, salt, and black pepper in a large bowl. Remove the potatoes from the oven, and add to the crème fraîche mixture. Add the chives and parsley, tossing gently to coat.

This salad, which is a perfect holiday dish, can also be served warm.

roasted vegetable salad WITH apple cider vinaigrette

///

SERVES **8 TO 10**   HANDS-ON TIME: **35 MINUTES**   TOTAL TIME: **3 HOURS, 55 MINUTES, INCLUDES CHILLING**

APPLE CIDER VINAIGRETTE:

¾ cup extra-virgin olive oil

¼ cup apple cider

¼ cup apple cider vinegar

2 tablespoons finely chopped shallots

1 tablespoon whole-grain Dijon mustard

1 tablespoon honey

1½ teaspoons kosher salt

1 teaspoon fresh thyme leaves

½ teaspoon freshly ground black pepper

1 pound parsnips, peeled and cut lengthwise

1 pound carrots, peeled and cut lengthwise

1 pound small golden beets, peeled and chopped

10 to 12 garlic cloves

1 cup frozen pearl onions, thawed

1 pound small Brussels sprouts, trimmed and halved

3 rosemary or thyme sprigs

3 small bay leaves

3 tablespoons butter, melted

1½ tablespoons olive oil

Kosher salt and freshly ground black pepper

1 head radicchio, separated into leaves

1 Make the Apple Cider Vinaigrette: Combine all the ingredients in a glass jar with a tight-fitting lid. Cover with the lid, and shake well. Shake the jar again just before serving.

2 Preheat the oven to 425°F.

3 Divide the parsnips, carrots, beets, garlic, onions, Brussels sprouts, rosemary or thyme sprigs, and bay leaves between 2 aluminum foil–lined jelly-roll pans. Drizzle with the butter and oil; toss to coat. Spread the vegetables in a single layer in each pan. Season with salt and pepper.

4 Bake both pans at 425°F for 20 minutes, placing 1 pan on the middle oven rack and 1 pan on the lower oven rack. Rotate the pans front to back, and top rack to bottom rack. Bake until the vegetables are tender, 20 to 25 more minutes.

5 Gently loosen the vegetables, and add the salt and pepper to taste. Cool completely, about 20 minutes. Discard the herb sprigs and bay leaves. Place the vegetables in a zip-top plastic freezer bag, and refrigerate 2 hours to 2 days.

6 To serve, let the vegetables stand 20 minutes or until room temperature. Add ¼ cup of the Apple Cider Vinaigrette; toss to coat.

7 Arrange the radicchio leaves on a serving platter; top with the roasted vegetables. Drizzle ¼ cup of the vinaigrette over the salad. Season with the salt and pepper. Serve the salad with the remaining vinaigrette.

We might as well call this "Kitchen Sink Winter Vegetables" as any of the cool-weather vegetables can be used—turnips, radishes, cabbage wedges, beets, and carrots to name a few.

roasted winter vegetables WITH miso vinaigrette

SERVES **8**   HANDS-ON TIME: **35 MINUTES**   TOTAL TIME: **1 HOUR, 5 MINUTES**

4 pounds winter vegetables (such as butternut squash, white and sweet potatoes, Brussels sprouts, and parsnips), peeled and trimmed as necessary and cut into 1-inch pieces (about 8 cups)

3 tablespoons extra-virgin olive oil

1 teaspoon kosher salt

2 teaspoons Asian sesame oil

¼ cup rice vinegar

3 tablespoons white miso

1 tablespoon soy sauce

2 tablespoons honey

2 tablespoons sesame seeds, toasted

3 scallions, thinly sliced

1 Preheat the oven to 400°F with racks in the upper and lower thirds.

2 Line 2 rimmed baking sheets with parchment paper.

3 Toss together the vegetables with the olive oil and salt in a large bowl. Divide the vegetables evenly between the prepared baking sheets, spreading them out in a single layer. Bake at 400°F, stirring occasionally and switching the baking sheets halfway through, until tender and very browned, 30 to 40 minutes.

4 Whisk together the sesame oil, rice vinegar, miso, soy sauce, and honey in a small bowl.

5 Remove the vegetables from the oven and transfer to a serving bowl. Immediately toss with the miso vinaigrette. Sprinkle the sesame seeds and scallions on top.

flavor note

The sweet and sour miso vinaigrette is the right complement to brighten the earthy and bitter vegetables. You can also use this vinaigrette as a topping for noodles or a mixed green salad, or as a marinade for mushrooms.

pizza
&bread

Hold the pizza sauce for this easy one-sheet pizza.

white pizza WITH salami AND peppers

SERVES **6**   HANDS-ON TIME: **35 MINUTES**   TOTAL TIME: **1 HOUR, 10 MINUTES**

1 pound refrigerated fresh pizza dough

8 ounces ricotta cheese (about 1 cup)

1 ounce mozzarella cheese, shredded (about ¼ cup)

1 garlic clove, minced

1 teaspoon kosher salt, plus more to taste

¼ teaspoon freshly ground black pepper, plus more to taste

3 tablespoons extra-virgin olive oil

8 slices salami, cut into strips

1 small yellow bell pepper, thinly sliced

1 small red bell pepper, thinly sliced

⅓ cup thinly sliced red onion

3 cups fresh arugula

1 teaspoon fresh lemon juice

¼ teaspoon crushed red pepper

1 Place a large baking sheet (at least 17- x 11-inches) in the oven. Preheat the oven to 450°F (keep the pan in the oven as it preheats).

2 Place the pizza dough on a lightly floured surface, and cover with plastic wrap. Let stand 20 minutes.

3 Stir together the cheeses, garlic, salt, pepper, and 2 tablespoons of the olive oil.

4 Carefully remove the preheated baking sheet from the oven. Roll out the dough on a floured surface to a 17- x 11-inch rectangle. Transfer to a large piece of lightly greased parchment paper; carefully place on the hot baking sheet. Top with the ricotta mixture, salami, bell peppers, and red onion. Brush the edges with ½ tablespoon of the olive oil.

5 Bake at 450°F until the dough is golden brown and crisp, 15 to 18 minutes.

6 Toss together the arugula, lemon juice, remaining ½ tablespoon olive oil, and salt and pepper to taste. Top the pizza with the arugula mixture; sprinkle with the crushed red pepper. Cut into 6 rectangles.

prep pointer

Preheating the baking sheet is key to achieving a crisp, crunchy, pizzeria-worthy crust at home.

Smoky bacon, rich walnuts, and woodsy thyme give depth to these quick personal pizzas. Cook the bacon in the oven using our Prep Pointer on page 29, or use leftover cooked bacon.

apple AND bacon pita pizzas

SERVES **4**   HANDS-ON TIME: **5 MINUTES**   TOTAL TIME: **7 MINUTES**

4 (6-inch) whole-wheat pitas

2 teaspoons olive oil

2 ounces Cheddar cheese, shredded (about ½ cup)

2 cups thinly sliced Fuji apple

3 tablespoons grated Parmesan cheese

2 tablespoons chopped walnuts, toasted

1 teaspoon chopped fresh thyme

2 applewood-smoked bacon slices, cooked and chopped

1 Preheat the broiler to high.

2 Broil the pitas directly on the oven rack 1 minute or until lightly golden. Remove from the oven and place on a large aluminum foil–lined baking sheet; carefully flip the pitas over. Brush evenly with the olive oil. Sprinkle the Cheddar over the pitas; arrange the apple slices over the cheese.

3 Sprinkle the Parmesan, walnuts, thyme, and bacon evenly over the apples. Return to the oven; broil 1 to 2 minutes.

flavor note

If you're a fan of pesto, spread some over each pita instead of olive oil for an added savory bite.

Apples star in this sweet-savory flatbread recipe—perfect for a light meal or the kids' lunches.

apple flatbread

SERVES **4 TO 8**   HANDS-ON TIME: **15 MINUTES**   TOTAL TIME: **35 MINUTES**

1 (11-ounce) can refrigerated thin-crust pizza dough

2 crisp, sweet apples (such as Gala, Fuji, or Braeburn)

1½ teaspoons fresh lemon juice

8 ounces ricotta cheese (about 1 cup)

1 teaspoon firmly packed grated lemon rind

½ teaspoon kosher salt

¼ teaspoon freshly ground black pepper

½ small red onion, thinly sliced

½ cup slivered almonds, toasted

1 teaspoon honey

Thinly sliced fresh flat-leaf parsley leaves (optional)

1 Preheat the oven to 425°F.

2 Press the pizza dough into a 14- x 9-inch rectangle on a jelly-roll pan lightly greased with cooking spray.

3 Bake at 425°F on the lower oven rack until lightly browned and crisp, 20 minutes. Meanwhile, thinly slice the apples, and toss with ½ teaspoon of the lemon juice.

4 Stir together the ricotta cheese, lemon rind, kosher salt, freshly ground black pepper, and remaining 1 teaspoon lemon juice. Spread the ricotta mixture over the baked crust.

5 Arrange the apples over the ricotta mixture, and sprinkle with the onion slices and almonds. Drizzle with the honey. Garnish with the parsley, if desired. Cut into squares. Serve immediately.

flavor note

For a variation, prepare the recipe through Step 2. Omit the ricotta, rind, onion, almonds, and honey. Cook 1 (12-ounce) package smoked chicken-and-apple sausage links according to the package directions for using a microwave or oven; slice. Stir the salt and pepper into ½ cup whipped cream cheese spread; spread over the baked crust. Top with the apples and sausage. Sprinkle with chopped fresh chives and basil.

Bagel halves are a quick, kid-friendly stand-in for traditional pizza crust. Since the pizzas are supereasy to make, this recipe is ideal for teaching kids to cook.

cheesy chicken bagel pizzas

SERVES **4**   HANDS-ON TIME: **5 MINUTES**   TOTAL TIME: **9 MINUTES**

2 (4½-inch, 2¼-ounce) plain bagels, sliced in half
½ cup marinara sauce
1 cup shredded skinless, boneless rotisserie chicken breast
4 ounces preshredded mozzarella cheese (about 1 cup)

1 Preheat the broiler.

2 Place the bagel halves, cut sides up, on a baking sheet. Broil until lightly toasted, 2 minutes.

3 Spread 2 tablespoons of the marinara on the cut side of each bagel half. Top each half with ¼ cup of the chicken, and sprinkle with ¼ cup of the cheese. Broil the bagel halves, until the cheese melts, 2 more minutes.

flavor note

Try onion- or cheese-flavored bagels for a tasty twist.

Using prepared chicken and commercial pizza crust gets this recipe on the table in 15 minutes. Serve at your next Tex-Mex–inspired dinner party.

southwestern bbq chicken pizza

SERVES **4 TO 6**   HANDS-ON TIME: **5 MINUTES**   TOTAL TIME: **15 MINUTES**

1 (16-ounce) Italian cheese-flavored pizza crust (such as Boboli)

½ cup barbecue sauce

2 (9-ounce) packages already-cooked Southwest-flavored chicken breast strips, chopped (such as Tyson)

6 ounces preshredded Mexican four-cheese blend (about 1½ cups)

2 tablespoons chopped fresh cilantro

1 Preheat the oven to 450°F.

2 Place the crust on a large baking sheet; spread ¼ cup of the barbecue sauce over the crust.

3 Combine the remaining ¼ cup barbecue sauce and chicken in a bowl, coating well. Spoon the chicken mixture over the crust; top with the cheese and cilantro.

4 Bake at 450°F until the cheese melts, 10 minutes. Cut into wedges.

Red onion, bell pepper, and plum tomatoes give this quick and easy pizza loads of fresh flavor. (Also pictured on page 150)

bbq chicken AND blue cheese pizza

SERVES **6**   HANDS-ON TIME: **10 MINUTES**   TOTAL TIME: **20 MINUTES**

1 (8-ounce) prebaked thin pizza crust (such as Mama Mary's)
⅓ cup barbecue sauce
1½ cups shredded skinless, boneless rotisserie chicken breast
½ cup vertically sliced red onion
½ cup coarsely chopped yellow bell pepper
2 ounces blue cheese, crumbled (about ½ cup)
2 plum tomatoes, thinly sliced
Fresh basil leaves (optional)

1 Preheat the oven to 500°F.

2 Place the pizza crust on a baking sheet. Spread the sauce over the crust, leaving a ½-inch border. Top with the chicken and next 4 ingredients. Bake at 500°F until the cheese melts and the crust is crisp, 10 minutes. Cut into 12 wedges. Garnish with the basil leaves, if desired.

flavor note

For a kid-friendly pie, substitute fresh mozzarella for the blue cheese.

This fresh spin on the classic sandwich will delight everyone at your table. Pair with a fresh salad or simple soup and serve for lunch.

turkey club pizza

SERVES **6**   HANDS-ON TIME: **20 MINUTES**   TOTAL TIME: **40 MINUTES**

1 (11-ounce) can refrigerated thin-crust pizza dough

¼ cup mayonnaise

3 tablespoons refrigerated pesto

2 cups cubed cooked turkey (such as Butterball Fully Cooked Oven Baked Turkey)

2 plum tomatoes, thinly sliced

¼ cup thinly sliced red onion

6 ounces Colby Jack cheese, shredded (about 1½ cups)

4 cooked and crumbled bacon slices

Ripe avocado, chopped

1 Preheat the oven to 450°F.

2 Unroll the dough; pat to an even thickness on a lightly greased baking sheet. Bake at 450°F until lightly browned, 10 to 12 minutes.

3 Stir together the mayonnaise and pesto sauce; spread evenly over the crust. Top with the turkey, tomatoes, and onion. Bake at 450°F for 6 to 8 minutes. Sprinkle with the cheese and bacon. Bake until the cheese melts. Top with the avocado. Cut into squares.

prep pointer

You can substitute the cooked and crumbled bacon for bacon bits, if you don't have leftover cooked bacon to use. One tablespoon of bacon bits is approximately 1½ strips of cooked bacon. You can also make a big batch of oven-cooked bacon (see the Prep Pointer on page 29) and then chop, package, and freeze it so that you always have cooked and crumbled bacon on hand.

This fresh pizza bursting with summer's best flavors is sure to become a family favorite. Letting the salt rest on the tomatoes for 20 minutes allows the salt to dissolve into the juicy flesh, making each bite even more piquant.

tomato AND corn pizza

SERVES **4**   HANDS-ON TIME: **10 MINUTES**   TOTAL TIME: **44 MINUTES**

3 small plum tomatoes, sliced
¼ teaspoon table salt
⅛ teaspoon freshly ground black pepper
1 (14-ounce) Italian cheese-flavored pizza crust
  (such as Boboli)
⅓ cup refrigerated pesto
½ cup fresh corn kernels
1 ounce Parmesan cheese, grated (about ¼ cup)
1 teaspoon sugar
8 ounces fresh mozzarella cheese, sliced
3 tablespoons fresh whole or torn basil leaves

1 Preheat the oven to 450°F.

2 Place the tomato slices on paper towels. Sprinkle evenly with the salt and pepper; let stand 20 minutes.

3 Place the pizza crust on a parchment paper–lined baking sheet; spread with the pesto. Stir together the corn, Parmesan, and sugar. Top the pizza with the corn mixture, tomatoes, and mozzarella slices.

4 Bake at 450°F until the cheese is melted and golden, 14 minutes. Remove from the oven, and top with the basil leaves. Cut into 4 wedges.

prep pointer

You can use thin crust prebaked pizza crust instead of the regular kind or use baked homemade pizza dough instead of the store-bought variety. See the subrecipe for Pizza Dough on page 170.

This nontraditional pizza uses potatoes for its crust, and the edges of the jelly-roll pan are essential in shaping it. Not only is this a surprising alternative to the standard wheat-based crust, but also it's gluten free.

potato-crusted pizza

SERVES **6**   HANDS-ON TIME: **10 MINUTES**   TOTAL TIME: **45 MINUTES**

1 tablespoon olive oil
1 (30-ounce) package frozen seasoned shredded
   potato rounds (such as Ore-Ida Crispy Crowns)
1 (28-ounce) can diced tomatoes, drained
1 (1-ounce) package fresh basil, torn
8 ounces preshredded pizza cheese blend
   (about 2 cups)

1 Preheat the oven to 450°F.

2 Brush a jelly-roll pan with the oil, and arrange the potatoes in a single layer on the pan. Bake at 450°F for 10 minutes. Flatten the potatoes, using the back of a wooden spoon, until the rounds touch and cover the entire pan. Bake 20 more minutes or until crisp. Top with the tomatoes, basil, and cheese blend. Bake until the cheese melts, 5 to 10 minutes. Cut into squares.

Make this tasty two-person tart and pair it with a hearty salad and red wine for a fun date night at home.

tomato-basil tart

SERVES **2**   HANDS-ON TIME: **10 MINUTES**   TOTAL TIME: **30 MINUTES**

1 sheet frozen puff pastry dough, thawed
4 tablespoons chopped fresh basil
3 ounces fresh mozzarella, grated (about ¾ cup)
1 ounce Parmesan, grated (about ¼ cup)
2 tablespoons jarred black olive tapenade
3 tomatoes, thinly sliced
½ teaspoon table salt
¼ teaspoon freshly ground black pepper

1 Preheat the oven to 425°F.

2 Line a jelly-roll pan with parchment paper.

3 On a lightly floured surface, roll out the thawed puff pastry to a 14- x 12-inch rectangle. Transfer the pastry to the prepared baking sheet. Brush the edges lightly with water. Fold them in to form a ½-inch border; press with a fork to seal all around. Prick the pastry all over with the fork.

4 Mix together 3 tablespoons of the chopped fresh basil, the mozzarella, and Parmesan. Spread the olive tapenade over the inside of the pastry. Sprinkle with the cheese-and-basil mixture; arrange the tomato slices decoratively on top. Sprinkle with the salt and pepper. Bake at 425°F until the crust is deep golden and the cheeses are melted, 20 to 25 minutes. Sprinkle with the remaining 1 tablespoon fresh basil. Cut into squares.

Scatter some chopped fresh oregano or parsley over the top this pizza just before serving for bright flavor and a splash of green.

roasted red pepper, feta, AND hummus pizza

SERVES **4**   HANDS-ON TIME: **20 MINUTES**   TOTAL TIME: **1 HOUR, 53 MINUTES, INCLUDES PIZZA DOUGH**

PIZZA DOUGH:

5.3 ounces all-purpose flour (1¼ cups)

1⅛ teaspoons (⅛ ounce) instant or rapid-rise dry yeast

½ teaspoon sugar

¼ teaspoon table salt

1 teaspoon extra-virgin olive oil

½ cup warm water (100° and 110°F)

HUMMUS:

1 large clove garlic, peeled

1 cup canned chickpeas, drained and rinsed

1 tablespoon tahini

1 tablespoon fresh lemon juice

½ teaspoon table salt

⅛ teaspoon freshly ground black pepper

2 tablespoons water

Cornmeal, for dusting

3 tablespoons extra-virgin olive oil

¼ cup ¼-inch-thick sliced roasted red peppers

2 ounces feta, crumbled (about ½ cup)

4 pitted large black olives, sliced

⅛ teaspoon crushed red pepper

¼ small red onion, thinly sliced

1 Make the Pizza Dough: Put the flour, yeast, sugar, and salt into the bowl of a food processor and pulse once or twice to mix. Combine the oil and warm water in a small glass measuring cup. With the food processor running, slowly pour the water mixture through the feed tube; process until a ball of dough forms. Let it run until the dough is smooth, about 1 minute. The dough should be slightly tacky but not too sticky. If necessary, add a little flour, 1 tablespoon at a time, and let it run for a little longer.

2 Oil a medium-sized bowl. Form the dough into a ball and transfer to the bowl, turning the dough to coat with the oil. Cover the bowl with plastic wrap or a clean kitchen towel and place in a warm place (85°F), free from drafts, until the dough doubles in size, about 45 minutes.

3 Meanwhile, place the oven rack on the lowest position. Place a large baking sheet on the rack. Preheat the oven to 550°F, or to your oven's highest temperature, for 45 minutes.

4 Make the Hummus: With the motor running, drop the garlic into the feed tube of the (cleaned) food processor. Scrape down the sides of the bowl. Add the chickpeas, tahini, lemon juice, salt, pepper, and water. Puree until smooth.

5 Make the Pizza: Dust a 14-inch-wide pizza peel with the cornmeal and flatten the dough on top.

Using lightly floured fingers or a floured rolling pin, stretch the dough into a 13- to 14-inch round. (Sprinkle the peel with more cornmeal if necessary to make sure the crust slides around easily on the peel.) Brush 1½ tablespoons of the oil over the crust.

6 Spread the Hummus over the crust, leaving a 1-inch border. Scatter the peppers, feta, olives, and crushed red pepper over the pizza. Drizzle the remaining 1½ tablespoons oil over the pizza.

7 Carefully slide the pizza onto the preheated baking sheet. Bake at 550°F until the crust is golden brown on the edges and on the bottom (lift an edge to check) and the cheese is lightly browned, about 8 minutes. Transfer to a cutting board. Sprinkle the onion slices over the pizza. Let rest for 1 minute. Cut into squares and serve.

pizza & bread

You can make this pizza ahead and freeze it until you're ready to eat it.

roasted asparagus, mushroom, AND onion pizza

SERVES **8**   HANDS-ON TIME: **51 MINUTES**   TOTAL TIME: **1 HOUR, 34 MINUTES**

1½ pounds refrigerated fresh pizza dough
2 pounds cremini mushrooms, quartered
2 small red onions, each cut into 12 wedges
Cooking spray
1 pound asparagus, trimmed and cut into thirds
2 tablespoons cornmeal
⅔ cup marinara sauce (such as Dell'Amore)
5 ounces fresh mozzarella cheese, torn into small
    pieces (about 1¼ cups)
3 ounces fontina cheese, shredded (about ¾ cup)
1½ tablespoons extra-virgin olive oil
1½ tablespoons balsamic vinegar
¾ teaspoon crushed red pepper
¼ cup fresh basil leaves
¼ teaspoon kosher salt

1 Divide the dough in half. Let stand at room temperature, covered, for 30 minutes.

2 Meanwhile, place 2 heavy baking sheets in the oven. Preheat the oven to 500°F (do not remove the baking sheets).

3 Combine the mushrooms and onions on a baking sheet; coat with the cooking spray. Bake at 500°F for 15 minutes. Add the asparagus to the pan; bake at 500°F for 15 minutes. Remove from the oven; cool.

4 Roll each piece of dough into a 15- x 9-inch rectangle on a lightly floured work surface. Carefully remove the baking sheets from the oven; sprinkle with the cornmeal. Arrange the dough on the baking sheets; coat with the cooking spray. Bake at 500°F for 8 minutes. Spread ⅓ cup of the sauce over each crust, leaving a ½-inch border. Top evenly with the vegetable mixture and the cheeses. Bake at 500°F for 5 to 6 more minutes.

5 Combine the oil, vinegar, and pepper in a small bowl; drizzle evenly over each pizza. Sprinkle with the basil and salt. Cut each pizza into 8 pieces.

prep pointer

Cool the partially baked pizza completely; wrap it tightly in heavy-duty aluminum foil. Freeze up to 2 months. When ready to eat, unwrap the pizza; bake directly on the oven rack at 450°F for 20 minutes or until browned and crisp. Top with the oil mixture, basil, and salt.

Lorraine cheese, which comes in long slices, is similar in flavor to Swiss cheese. If you don't have fresh oregano, you can substitute ½ teaspoon dried oregano.

roasted mushroom AND shallot pizza

SERVES **6**   HANDS-ON TIME: **20 MINUTES**   TOTAL TIME: **43 MINUTES**

ROASTED MUSHROOMS AND SHALLOTS:

1 tablespoon extra-virgin olive oil

¼ teaspoon table salt

¾ teaspoon freshly ground black pepper

4 garlic cloves, minced

1 (8-ounce) package baby portobello mushrooms, quartered

1 (3.5-ounce) package shiitake mushrooms, stems removed and quartered

2 (3-ounce) packages small shallots, peeled and quartered lengthwise

½ (8-ounce) tub chive-and-onion cream cheese

1 (10-ounce) Italian cheese-flavored thin pizza crust (such as Boboli)

3 (1-ounce) slices Lorraine cheese (such as Saputo)

2 tablespoons fresh oregano leaves

1 Preheat the oven to 450°F.

2 Make the Roasted Mushrooms and Shallots: Combine the olive oil, salt, black pepper, and garlic in a large bowl. Add the mushrooms and shallots; toss to coat. Spread the mushroom mixture in a single layer on a jelly-roll pan lightly coated with cooking spray. Bake at 450° for 15 minutes (do not stir).

3 Spread the cream cheese over the pizza crust. Top with the Roasted Mushrooms and Shallots and the cheese slices.

4 Bake the pizza directly on the oven rack at 450°F until the crust is golden and the cheese melts, 8 minutes. Sprinkle with the oregano. Cut into wedges, and serve immediately.

If you love a loaded pizza, try this recipe. A whole-wheat crust topped with roasted sweet potatoes and other colorful veggies makes it a hearty meal.

roasted vegetable pizza

SERVES **4**   HANDS-ON TIME: **25 MINUTES**   TOTAL TIME: **1 HOUR, 55 MINUTES**

1 medium eggplant, peeled and cubed

¼ teaspoon table salt, plus more to taste

2 medium zucchini, sliced

1 large sweet potato, peeled and cut into ½-inch cubes

1 onion, peeled and cut into eighths

1 red bell pepper, cut into 1-inch pieces

¼ cup plus 1 teaspoon olive oil

1 tablespoon chopped fresh rosemary

¼ teaspoon freshly ground black pepper

½ (16-ounce) package whole-wheat prebaked pizza crusts (such as Mama Mary's)

1.3 ounces Asiago cheese, shaved (about ⅓ cup)

1 Sprinkle the eggplant with the ¼ teaspoon salt, and let stand 30 minutes. Pat dry.

2 Preheat the oven to 400°F.

3 Toss together the eggplant, zucchini, sweet potato, onion, bell pepper, ¼ cup of the oil, rosemary, and black pepper; arrange in a single layer on 2 aluminum foil–lined jelly-roll pans.

4 Bake at 400°F until the vegetables are tender and golden brown, 45 minutes. Season with salt to taste.

5 Place the pizza crust on a baking sheet. Brush the crust with the remaining 1 teaspoon oil. Top with 2 cups of the roasted vegetables; reserve the remaining vegetables for another use. Sprinkle with the cheese. Bake at 400°F until the crust is crisp and the cheese is melted, 15 minutes. Cut into wedges.

prep pointer

You will have leftover roasted vegetables. Refrigerate them overnight and reheat the next day for a delicious lunch at work.

Keep it easy: Roll the dough out on a large piece of parchment paper, and place the paper right on the hot baking sheet.

zucchini-ricotta pizza

SERVES **4**   HANDS-ON TIME: **25 MINUTES**   TOTAL TIME: **50 MINUTES, NOT INCLUDING PIZZA DOUGH**

1 pint cherry tomatoes, halved

1 tablespoon canola oil

1 portion Pizza Dough (page 88)

6 ounces ricotta cheese (about ¾ cup)

3 tablespoons finely chopped fresh basil

2 tablespoons finely chopped fresh mint

2 tablespoons milk

1 garlic clove, grated

2 medium zucchini, shaved

2 ounces feta cheese, crumbled (½ cup)

1 Place a baking sheet in the oven. Preheat the oven to 500°F (do not remove the baking sheet from the oven).

2 Combine the tomatoes and 1½ teaspoons of the canola oil on another aluminum foil–lined baking sheet. Bake at 500°F for 7 minutes.

3 Roll the dough portion into a 13-inch circle on a work surface; pierce well with a fork. Carefully place on the preheated baking sheet. Bake at 500°F for 4 minutes. Combine the remaining ¼ teaspoon salt, ricotta, basil, mint, milk, and garlic; spread over the dough, leaving a ½-inch border. Combine the zucchini and the remaining 1½ teaspoons canola oil; arrange on the pizza. Top the pizza with the feta. Bake at 500°F for 10 minutes. Top with the tomatoes; bake at 500°F for 4 minutes. Cut into 8 wedges.

prep pointer

The Pizza Dough on page 88 makes 3 portions. You only need 1 portion for this recipe. If you're using a reserved dough portion that has been frozen, thaw it in the refrigerator for at least 12 hours, and then let it come to room temperature for 30 minutes before using.

Savory scones are a delightful alternative to a typically sweet treat. This is another recipe where those handy tricks of cooking bacon in the oven (see Prep Pointer on page 29) or subbing cooked bacon with bacon bits (see Prep Pointer on page 162) are helpful.

bacon, cheddar, AND chives scones

MAKES **8 SCONES**   HANDS-ON TIME: **15 MINUTES**   TOTAL TIME: **33 MINUTES**

8½ ounces all-purpose flour (about 2 cups)

1 tablespoon baking powder

½ teaspoon table salt

8 tablespoons cold butter (1 stick), cut into ½-inch cubes

1 cup whipping cream

3 ounces sharp Cheddar cheese, shredded (about ¾ cup)

¼ cup finely chopped cooked bacon

2 tablespoons chopped fresh chives

½ teaspoon freshly ground black pepper

1 Preheat the oven to 450°F.

2 Weigh or lightly spoon the flour into dry measuring cups; level with a knife. Stir together the flour, baking powder, and salt in a large bowl.

Cut the butter into the flour mixture with a pastry blender until crumbly and the mixture resembles small peas. Freeze 5 minutes. Add ¾ cup plus 2 tablespoons of the cream, cheese, bacon, chives, and pepper; stir just until the dry ingredients are moistened.

3 Turn the dough out onto wax paper; gently press or pat the dough into a 7-inch round (the mixture will be crumbly). Cut the round into 8 wedges. Place the wedges 2 inches apart on a lightly greased baking sheet. Brush the tops of the wedges with the remaining 2 tablespoons cream just until moistened.

4 Bake at 450°F until golden, 13 to 15 minutes.

prep pointer

Freezing the dough allows the butter to resolidify after being cut into the flour mixture. Maintaining solid chunks of cold butter rather than melted butter before baking is what gives scones and other pastries their flaky quality.

Precooked sausage is a time-saver in this recipe—simply chop the sausage, and add it to the dough along with the cheese. Try meatless breakfast sausage patties for a vegetarian option.

sausage drop scones

MAKES **15 SCONES**   HANDS-ON TIME: **10 MINUTES**   TOTAL TIME: **25 MINUTES**

3 cups baking mix (about 13 ounces)

1½ teaspoons freshly ground black pepper

2 tablespoons chilled butter, cut into small pieces

¾ cup evaporated milk

2 ounces Cheddar cheese with jalapeño chiles, shredded (about ½ cup)

4 fully cooked turkey breakfast sausage patties, chopped (such as Jimmy Dean Fully Cooked Turkey Sausage Patties)

Cooking spray

1 Preheat the oven to 425°F.

2 Combine the baking mix and black pepper in a large bowl. Cut in the butter with a pastry blender or 2 knives until the mixture resembles a coarse meal. Add the evaporated milk, cheese, and sausage; stir just until moist. Drop the dough by ¼ cupfuls onto a baking sheet lined with parchment paper. Coat the dough with the cooking spray.

3 Bake at 425°F until the scones are golden, about 15 minutes.

Day-old scones are firm enough to slice open without crumbling. Tuck in a few paper-thin slices of country ham for an unforgettable ham "biscuit."

spinach-feta scones

MAKES **8 SCONES**   HANDS-ON TIME: **20 MINUTES**   TOTAL TIME: **40 MINUTES**

10 ounces self-rising flour (about 2½ cups)

1 tablespoon sugar

8 tablespoons cold butter (1 stick), cut into ½-inch cubes

1 cup chopped fresh spinach

5.3 ounces feta cheese, crumbled (about 1 cup)

1¼ cups plus 2 tablespoons heavy cream

1 Preheat the oven to 450°F.

2 Weigh or lightly spoon the flour into dry measuring cups; level with a knife. Stir together the flour and sugar in a large bowl. Cut the butter into the flour mixture with a pastry blender until crumbly and the mixture resembles small peas. Freeze 5 minutes. Stir in the spinach and feta until combined. Add 1 cup of the cream, stirring just until the dry ingredients are moistened. Stir in up to ¼ cup more cream, 1 tablespoon at a time, if needed.

3 Turn the dough out onto lightly floured wax paper; gently press or pat the dough into an 8-inch round (the mixture will be crumbly). Cut the round into 8 wedges. Place the wedges 2 inches apart on a parchment paper–lined baking sheet. Brush the tops with the remaining 2 tablespoons cream just until moistened.

4 Bake at 450°F until golden, 14 to 16 minutes.

prep pointer

Dip the knife into flour before cutting the scones to prevent the dough from sticking to the knife. When you cut the wedges, don't cut all the way through the dough; instead, keep a thin bottom layer of dough intact. Keeping the wedges in close proximity will prevent them from drying out during baking.

Nutmeg, cardamom, ginger, and sweet potato combine to create scones loaded with comforting flavor. Serve these with tea or coffee for breakfast or when a friend comes to visit.

sweet potato–ginger scones

MAKES **16 SCONES**   HANDS-ON TIME: **20 MINUTES**   TOTAL TIME: **55 MINUTES**

1 pound, 5¼ ounces all-purpose flour, plus more for baking sheet (about 5 cups)

⅔ cup granulated sugar

1 ½ tablespoons baking powder

1 teaspoon kosher salt

⅛ teaspoon grated whole nutmeg

⅝ teaspoon ground cardamom

24 tablespoons (3 sticks) very cold unsalted butter, cut into ½-inch pieces

½ cup chopped crystallized ginger

2 teaspoons lemon rind

1 cup chilled mashed roasted sweet potato

¾ cup cold buttermilk

¼ cup plus 2 tablespoons heavy cream

¼ cup turbinado sugar

1 Preheat the oven to 400°F.

2 Line a baking sheet with parchment paper.

3 Weigh or lightly spoon the flour into dry measuring cups; level with a knife. Sift together the flour, sugar, baking powder, salt, nutmeg, and ½ teaspoon of the cardamom. Add the butter; cut into the flour mixture with a pastry blender or a fork until the butter pieces are the size of corn kernels. Stir in the ginger and rind.

Stir together the sweet potatoes, buttermilk, and ¼ cup of the cream in a small bowl. Make a well in the center of the flour mixture; place the sweet potato mixture in the well. Working quickly, stir until the dough just comes together.

4 Sprinkle the prepared baking sheet liberally with the flour. Place the dough on the parchment, and divide the dough in half. With floured hands, shape each dough half into a circle between 6 and 7 inches in diameter and about 1 inch thick. Brush the circles evenly with the remaining 2 tablespoons cream. Stir together the turbinado sugar and the remaining ⅛ teaspoon cardamom in a small bowl, and sprinkle evenly over the dough circles. Run a bread knife or bench scraper under cold water, and cut each circle into 8 wedges. Carefully pull the wedges away from the center to separate them by about ¾ inch.

5 Bake on the middle rack at 400°F until golden brown and almost cooked through, about 30 minutes. Transfer the baking sheet to the lowest oven rack; bake until the bottoms of the scones are fully cooked, about 5 minutes. Serve warm or at room temperature.

pizza & bread

Serve these decadent rolls at a tea, a shower, or a holiday brunch.

cinnamon-pecan rolls

MAKES **1 DOZEN ROLLS**   HANDS-ON TIME: **35 MINUTES**   TOTAL TIME: **1 HOUR**

14⅞ ounces all-purpose flour (about 3½ cups)
3 tablespoons granulated sugar
1½ teaspoons baking powder
½ teaspoon baking soda
½ teaspoon kosher salt
1½ cups buttermilk
6 tablespoons unsalted butter, melted
1½ teaspoons vanilla extract
¼ cup packed dark brown sugar
1½ teaspoons ground cinnamon
¾ cup coarsely chopped pecans
4 ounces cream cheese, softened
1 cup (about 4 ounces) powdered sugar
4 tablespoons unsalted butter, softened
1 to 2 teaspoons whole milk

1 Preheat the oven to 400°F.

2 Line a baking sheet with parchment paper. Weigh or lightly spoon 3 cups of the flour into dry measuring cups; level with a knife. Stir together the flour, granulated sugar, baking powder, baking soda, and salt in a medium bowl. Stir together the buttermilk, 5 tablespoons of the melted butter, and 1 teaspoon of the vanilla in a small bowl. Add the buttermilk mixture to the flour mixture, and stir to combine.

3 Sprinkle ¼ cup of the flour on a work surface; turn out the dough, and sprinkle with the remaining ¼ cup flour. Knead lightly.

4 Using a lightly floured rolling pin, roll the dough into a 12-inch square about ¼ inch thick. Brush the dough with the remaining 1 tablespoon melted butter. Sprinkle with the brown sugar, cinnamon, and ½ cup of the pecans. Roll the dough into a log, starting with edge closest to you. Pinch the seam closed.

5 Using a very sharp or serrated knife, cut the log into 1-inch-thick slices. Transfer the slices to the prepared baking sheet. Bake at 400°F until golden brown, 25 to 30 minutes. (Cover with aluminum foil at the end of baking if the exposed pecans start to darken too much.)

6 Meanwhile, stir together the cream cheese, powdered sugar, softened butter, 1 teaspoon milk, and remaining ½ teaspoon vanilla in a medium bowl. Beat with an electric mixer at medium speed until smooth. (Add up to 1 teaspoon more milk, ½ teaspoon at a time, and beat until the desired consistency is reached.) Spread the glaze over the warm rolls. Top with the remaining ¼ cup pecans.

Make these your go-to rolls for dinner. Eat them with Honey-Pecan Chicken Thighs (page 85) and a side salad for a delicious simple meal.

hurry-up homemade crescent rolls

MAKES **1 DOZEN ROLLS**   HANDS-ON TIME: **25 MINUTES**   TOTAL TIME: **1 HOUR, 35 MINUTES**

1 (¼-ounce) envelope active dry yeast
¾ cup warm water (100° to 110°F)
3 to 3½ cups baking mix (about 13 to 15 ounces)
2 tablespoons sugar
¼ teaspoon kosher salt

1 Combine the yeast and warm water in a 1-cup measuring cup; let stand 5 minutes. Combine 3 cups of the baking mix and sugar in a large bowl; gradually stir in the yeast mixture.

2 Turn the dough out onto a floured surface, and knead, adding additional baking mix (up to ½ cup) as needed, until the dough is smooth and elastic (about 10 minutes).

3 Roll the dough into a 12-inch circle; cut the circle into 12 wedges. Roll up the wedges, starting at the wide end, to form a crescent shape; place, point sides down, on a lightly greased baking sheet. Cover and let rise in a warm place (85°F), free from drafts, 1 hour or until doubled in size.

4 Preheat the oven to 425°F. Bake until golden, 10 to 12 minutes. Sprinkle evenly with the kosher salt.

prep pointer

These rolls may be frozen up to 2 months. To freeze, bake at 425°F for 5 minutes; cool completely (about 30 minutes). Wrap in aluminum foil, and freeze in an airtight container. Thaw at room temperature on a lightly greased baking sheet; bake at 425°F until golden, 7 to 8 minutes.

Rye flour and hazelnuts have a distinct rich flavor that makes these rolls anything but an afterthought. Make ahead, and freeze up to 1 month.

hazelnut-rye rolls

MAKES **16 ROLLS**   HANDS-ON TIME: **25 MINUTES**   TOTAL TIME: **2 HOURS, 24 MINUTES**

1 cup milk
1 tablespoon honey
1 package active dry yeast (about 2¼ teaspoons)
2 tablespoons olive oil
9½ ounces bread flour (about 2 cups)
3½ ounces light rye flour (about 1 cup)
¼ cup chopped hazelnuts, toasted
1½ teaspoons table salt
1 tablespoon water
1 large egg white, lightly beaten

1 Microwave ¼ cup of the milk in a microwave-safe measuring cup at MEDIUM for 30 seconds or until warm. Combine the milk, honey, and yeast in the bowl of a stand mixer fitted with the dough hook. Let stand 5 minutes or until the mixture is bubbly. Microwave the remaining ¾ cup milk in the microwave-safe measuring cup at MEDIUM for 30 seconds, or until warm. Stir in the remaining warm milk and olive oil.

2 Weigh or lightly spoon 3 ounces (1¾ cups) of the bread flour and the rye flour into dry measuring cups; level with a knife. Add the flour mixture, hazelnuts, and salt to the stand mixer; mix at medium-low speed just until combined.

With the mixer at low speed, gradually add the remaining 2 ounces (¼ cup) bread flour. Mix at low speed 5 minutes or until a soft dough forms, scraping the sides of the bowl once. Place the dough in a bowl coated with cooking spray, turning to coat. Cover and let rise in a warm place (85°F), free from drafts, 1 hour or until doubled in size.

3 Punch the dough down; turn out onto a lightly floured surface. Cut the dough into 16 equal pieces. Working with 1 piece at a time, roll the dough into a ball by cupping your hand and pushing against the dough and surface while rolling. Arrange the dough balls 1 inch apart on a baking sheet coated with cooking spray. Cover and let rise 45 minutes or until the dough is doubled in size.

4 Preheat the oven to 375°F.

5 Combine the water and egg white in a small bowl; brush evenly over the rolls. Bake at 375°F until golden, 14 minutes. Remove the rolls from the pan; cool on a wire rack.

Don't put this bread under the broiler and walk away—it browns in only 2 minutes! Every oven is different, so be sure to keep an eye on it.

asiago-topped garlic bread

//

MAKES **1 DOZEN BREAD SLICES**   HANDS-ON TIME: **6 MINUTES**   TOTAL TIME: **8 MINUTES**

1½ tablespoons olive oil vinaigrette
1 garlic clove, minced
1 (9-ounce) whole-wheat baguette, diagonally cut
    into 12 slices
2 ounces Asiago cheese, grated (½ cup)
½ teaspoon chopped fresh rosemary

1 Preheat the broiler.

2 Combine the vinaigrette and garlic in a small bowl; spread evenly over the tops of the bread slices. Sprinkle with the cheese and rosemary.

3 Place the bread on a baking sheet. Broil until the cheese melts and the bread is lightly browned, 2 minutes.

flavor note

There are many pleasing herbs and spices that can top this bread. Try a dash of crushed red pepper, onion powder, or Italian seasoning instead of (or in addition to) the rosemary.

A rich, tender, herb-filled biscuit slab cradles just-right, over-easy eggs drizzled with hot sauce and a sprinkled with fresh parsley. Serve the biscuits with sweet accompaniments, such as jam and honey butter.

ricotta-chive biscuits WITH baked eggs

SERVES 4   HANDS-ON TIME: **20 MINUTES**   TOTAL TIME: **46 MINUTES**

2½ cups (about 11⅞ ounces) soft winter wheat self-rising flour (such as White Lily), plus more for dusting

8 tablespoons salted butter (1 stick), chilled and cut into cubes

3 tablespoons chopped fresh chives

¾ cup whole buttermilk, chilled

¼ cup ricotta cheese, chilled

4 large eggs

2 tablespoons salted butter, melted

1 tablespoon hot sauce (such as Cholula)

1 tablespoon chopped fresh flat-leaf parsley

1 Preheat the oven to 475°F.

2 Lightly dust a parchment paper-lined baking sheet with flour. Set aside.

3 Weigh or lightly spoon the flour into dry measuring cups; level with a knife. Place the flour in a large bowl. Add the cubed butter; cut into the flour with a pastry cutter until crumbly and the mixture resembles small peas. Stir in the chives. Chill 10 minutes. Whisk together the buttermilk and ricotta. Using a fork, gently stir the buttermilk mixture into the flour mixture just until incorporated.

4 Turn the dough out onto the prepared baking sheet. Press into a 10- x 6-inch rectangle. Fold in half so that short ends meet. Repeat the procedure of pressing the dough into a 10- x 6-inch rectangle and folding 3 times. Press the dough into a 10- x 6-inch rectangle. Using a 2 ¼-inch round cutter, cut 4 evenly spaced circles from the dough rectangle, leaving at least ½ inch between circles. Carefully remove the dough rounds, leaving the dough rectangle intact. Place the dough rounds on the edge of the baking sheet beside the dough rectangle. Bake at 475°F until the edges are lightly browned, 10 to 12 minutes.

5 Break the eggs into the circles in the biscuit rectangle. Return to the oven, and bake until the egg whites are set, 6 to 7 minutes.

6 Brush the biscuit rectangle and biscuit rounds evenly with the melted butter. Drizzle evenly with the hot sauce, and sprinkle with the parsley.

When the warm butter meets the cold buttermilk, it will begin to form clumps—little droplets of fat throughout the liquid—a sign of success. The pockets ensure even distribution of fat throughout the batter, creating a fluffy biscuit.

fluffy buttermilk drop biscuits

MAKES **1 DOZEN BISCUITS**   HANDS-ON TIME: **7 MINUTES**   TOTAL TIME: **21 MINUTES**

5.6 ounces unbleached all-purpose flour (about 1¼ cups)

3.6 ounces white whole-wheat flour (about ¾ cup)

2 teaspoons baking powder

1 teaspoon sugar

¾ teaspoon table salt

½ teaspoon baking soda

4 tablespoons unsalted butter

1¼ cups very cold buttermilk

1 tablespoon canola oil

1 Preheat the oven to 450°F.

2 Weigh or lightly spoon the flours into dry measuring cups; level with a knife. Combine the flours, baking powder, sugar, salt, and baking soda in a large bowl; whisk to combine.

3 Place the butter in a microwave-safe bowl. Microwave at HIGH for 1 minute or until completely melted. Add the cold buttermilk, stirring until the butter forms small clumps. Add the oil, stirring to combine.

4 Add the buttermilk mixture to the flour mixture; stir with a rubber spatula until just incorporated (do not overmix) and the batter pulls away from the sides of the bowl. (The batter will be very wet.)

5 Drop the batter in mounds of 2 heaping tablespoonfuls onto a baking sheet lined with parchment paper. Bake at 450°F until golden, 11 minutes. Cool 3 minutes. Serve warm.

Serve these biscuits for breakfast, as a side, or as an appetizer split and topped with your favorite meat—like pulled pork or rotisserie chicken—and drizzled with sauce.

sweet potato biscuits

MAKES **ABOUT 2 DOZEN BISCUITS**   HANDS-ON TIME: **20 MINUTES**   TOTAL TIME: **35 MINUTES**

1½ cups cooked mashed sweet potatoes (about 2½ sweet potatoes)
1 cup buttermilk
6 tablespoons butter, melted
2 tablespoons sugar
⅛ teaspoon baking soda
14 ounces self-rising flour (about 3⅓ cups)

1 Preheat the oven to 400°F.

2 Stir together the sweet potatoes, buttermilk, and butter in a large bowl. Add the sugar, baking soda, and 3 cups of the flour, stirring just until the dry ingredients are moistened.

3 Turn the dough out onto a lightly floured surface; knead 8 to 10 times, adding up to ⅓ cup more flour to prevent the dough from sticking. Roll the dough to ¾-inch thick; cut with a 2-inch round cutter. Place the biscuits on a baking sheet lightly coated with cooking spray.

4 Bake at 400°F until golden brown, about 15 to 20 minutes.

prep pointer

You can easily bake sweet potatoes in the microwave. Wash and dry the potatoes; pierce several times with a fork. Wrap each potato in a damp paper towel (this will create a steaming affect during cooking). Microwave at HIGH 5 to 10 minutes on a microwave-safe plate, flipping the potatoes halfway through. Let the potatoes cool; halve with a knife. Using a spoon, remove the cooked potato from the skin to a bowl, and mash.

Gently pat the dough flat instead of rolling with a rolling pin. Patting preserves all the pockets of fat needed for flaky biscuits, whereas rolling pancakes them into small, dense pucks. Cut the biscuits into squares to avoid any leftover scraps.

whole-grain spelt AND cornmeal biscuits

MAKES **16 BISCUITS**   HANDS-ON TIME: **15 MINUTES**   TOTAL TIME: **25 MINUTES**

11.25 ounces spelt flour (about 2½ cups)
2 ounces whole-grain cornmeal (about ½ cup)
2½ tablespoons baking powder
½ teaspoon baking soda
½ teaspoon kosher salt
8 tablespoons chilled unsalted butter (1 stick), cut into pieces
1 cup buttermilk

1 Preheat the oven to 450°F.

2 Weigh or lightly spoon the flour into dry measuring cups; level with a knife. Combine the flour, cornmeal, baking powder, baking soda, and salt in a bowl, stirring with a whisk. Cut the butter into the flour mixture using a pastry blender or 2 knives until the mixture resembles a coarse meal. Stir in the buttermilk just until combined.

3 Turn the dough out onto a lightly floured surface. Knead 2 to 3 times or until the dough comes together. Pat the dough into a 10- x 8-inch rectangle; cut into 16 squares. Place the biscuits 2 inches apart on a parchment paper–lined baking sheet. Bake at 450°F until browned, 10 to 12 minutes.

flavor note

Spelt flour adds a deep nutty flavor, but you can use white whole-wheat flour if you can't find spelt.

Bake these biscuits up to a day ahead, and keep in a sealed zip-top plastic bag.

orange, honey, AND thyme biscuits

MAKES **1 DOZEN BISCUITS**   HANDS-ON TIME: **7 MINUTES**   TOTAL TIME: **20 MINUTES**

⅔ cup buttermilk

2 tablespoons clover honey

2 teaspoons chopped fresh thyme

2 teaspoons grated orange rind

10 ounces spelt flour (about 2 cups)

5 teaspoons baking powder

¼ teaspoon kosher salt

5½ tablespoons chilled butter, cut into small pieces

1 Preheat the oven to 425°F.

2 Combine the buttermilk, honey, thyme, and rind in a small bowl, stirring with a whisk.

3 Weigh or lightly spoon the flour into dry measuring cups; level with a knife. Combine the flour, baking powder, and salt in a medium bowl, stirring with a whisk. Cut in the butter with a pastry blender or 2 knives until the mixture resembles a coarse meal. Add the buttermilk mixture to the flour mixture, stirring just until moist. Turn the dough out onto a lightly floured surface; pat into a 7½-inch square; cut into 12 rectangles. Place the dough on an aluminum foil–lined baking sheet coated with cooking spray. Bake at 425°F until lightly browned on the edges and bottom, 13 minutes.

flavor note

Clover honey, like all honeys, gets its name from the blossom from which it's harvested. Clover honey has a milder flavor than most other varieties and is the type most commonly sold in supermarkets.

soups
& spreads

This soup is a refreshing meal during the summer or early fall. Using a blender to puree the carrot juice with half of the cucumber mixture adds body to the soup. To cut down on prep time, leave out that step. (Also pictured on page 201)

curry-roasted carrot gazpacho

SERVES **6** HANDS-ON TIME: **20 MINUTES** TOTAL TIME: **1 HOUR**

3 large carrots, peeled and quartered lengthwise
1 large golden beet, peeled and cut into ½-inch slices
1 cup chopped white onion (1 medium onion)
3 tablespoons olive oil
2 teaspoons curry powder
1 teaspoon table salt
1 English cucumber, peeled and diced
1 yellow bell pepper, diced
1 large yellow tomato, diced
¼ cup white wine vinegar
½ teaspoon freshly ground white pepper
3 cups carrot juice
½ cup crème fraîche
¼ cup chopped fresh chives
½ teaspoon freshly ground black pepper

1 Preheat the oven to 375°F.

2 Place the carrots, beet, and onion on a half-sized baking sheet. Add the oil, curry powder, and ½ teaspoon of the salt; toss to coat. Bake at 375°F until the vegetables are tender and beginning to brown, 20 to 25 minutes, stirring after 15 minutes.

3 Scrape the vegetables and any accumulated pan juices into a large bowl; chill completely, about 20 minutes. Dice the carrots and beet, and return to the bowl.

4 Combine the cucumber, bell pepper, tomato, vinegar, white pepper, and the remaining ½ teaspoon salt in a separate bowl; stir gently to combine. Place the carrot juice and half of the cucumber mixture in a blender; process until smooth, 30 seconds to 1 minute. Add the processed cucumber mixture to the cucumber mixture in the bowl; stir to combine.

5 Ladle the cucumber mixture into each of 6 bowls; top each serving with the carrot mixture. Dollop each serving evenly with the crème fraîche, and sprinkle evenly with the chives and black pepper.

prep pointer

Beets come in a variety of sizes, so feel free to use several small beets or 1 (8- to 10-ounce) beet.

Serve this tasty soup at an al fresco dinner party with a bread-based appetizer like Pesto Pastries (page 19) that can be eaten separately or dipped into the gazpacho.

tomato gazpacho WITH garden vegetables

SERVES **6**   HANDS-ON TIME: **15 MINUTES**   TOTAL TIME: **30 MINUTES**

1 English cucumber, diced
1 large red bell pepper, diced
1 large red tomato, diced
2 celery stalks, finely chopped
1 cup chopped yellow onion (1 medium onion)
3 tablespoons olive oil
3 garlic cloves, peeled
3 cups vegetable juice, chilled
¼ cup red wine vinegar
1¼ teaspoons table salt
1 teaspoon freshly ground black pepper
3 tablespoons sour cream
2 tablespoons chopped fresh dill

1 Preheat the oven to 375°F.

2 Combine the cucumber, bell pepper, tomato, and celery in a medium bowl; stir to combine. Place half of the vegetable mixture on a half-sized baking sheet; set aside the remaining vegetable mixture. Add the onion, oil, and garlic to the vegetables on the baking sheet; stir to coat. Bake at 375°F until tender, 15 minutes.

3 Place the roasted vegetables, vegetable juice, vinegar, salt, and ½ teaspoon of the black pepper in a blender; process until very smooth, 30 seconds to 1 minute. Ladle the soup into each of 6 bowls. Top each serving evenly with the reserved cucumber mixture. Dollop the servings evenly with the sour cream, and sprinkle evenly with the dill and the reamining ½ teaspoon of the black pepper.

Think you need a stovetop to make hot, fresh soup? Think again! This easy soup, bursting with roasted veggie flavor, proves how useful your baking sheet really is. It is easy to double or make ahead and freeze until ready to eat. Top with fresh grated cheese and herbed croutons to up your game.

creamy tomato-vegetable soup

SERVES **4**   HANDS-ON TIME: **15 MINUTES**   TOTAL TIME: **50 MINUTES**

3 large plum tomatoes, halved lengthwise

1 cup roughly chopped yellow onion (1 medium onion)

1 small fennel bulb, trimmed and roughly chopped

1 large carrot, peeled and chopped

4 unpeeled garlic cloves

3 tablespoons olive oil

2 tablespoons tomato paste

1 tablespoon chopped fresh thyme

1 teaspoon table salt

½ teaspoon freshly ground black pepper

3 cups chicken stock

⅓ cup heavy cream

2 tablespoons red wine vinegar

¼ cup torn fresh flat-leaf parsley

1 Preheat the oven to 375°F.

2 Place the tomatoes (cut sides down), onion, fennel, carrot, and garlic cloves on a half-sized baking sheet coated with cooking spray. Stir together the oil and tomato paste in a small bowl. Add the oil mixture, thyme, ½ teaspoon of the salt, and ¼ teaspoon of the pepper to the tomato mixture; toss to coat. Bake at 375°F until the vegetables are tender and beginning to brown, about 35 minutes.

3 Squeeze the garlic from the cloves into a blender, discarding the skins. Scrape the vegetable mixture and any accumulated pan juices into the blender.

4 Combine the stock and cream in a large microwave-safe bowl; microwave at HIGH until hot, 2 to 3 minutes. Add the stock mixture, vinegar, and remaining ½ teaspoon salt and ¼ teaspoon pepper to the blender. Remove the center piece of the blender lid (to allow steam to escape); secure the blender lid on the blender. Place a clean towel over the opening in the blender lid (to avoid splatters). Process until very smooth, 30 seconds to 1 minute.

5 Carefully ladle the soup into each of 4 bowls; top the servings evenly with the parsley.

Hearty and savory, this is the perfect soup for a cold day. Leeks are an unexpected ingredient that lends pleasing earthiness and a mild onion-like flavor to the dish.

roasted potato AND leek soup

SERVES **6**   HANDS-ON TIME: **20 MINUTES**   TOTAL TIME: **1 HOUR, 14 MINUTES**

1 pound russet potato (about 1 large potato), peeled and chopped

1 pound Yukon Gold potatoes (about 4 medium potatoes), peeled and chopped

2 large leeks, trimmed and chopped

3 celery stalks, chopped leaves reserved

1 large lemon, quartered

¼ cup olive oil

1½ teaspoons table salt

½ teaspoon freshly ground black pepper

4 cups chicken stock

2 bay leaves

½ cup heavy cream

1 Preheat the oven to 375°F.

2 Place the potatoes, leeks, celery, and lemon wedges on a full-sized baking sheet. Add the oil, 1 teaspoon of the salt, and ¼ teaspoon of the pepper; toss to coat. Bake at 375°F until the vegetables are tender and beginning to brown, 30 to 35 minutes.

3 Squeeze the juice from the lemon wedges over the potato mixture; discard the lemons. Scrape the potato mixture and any accumulated pan juices into a blender. Add 2 cups of the stock; process until smooth, about 1 minute.

4 Place the bay leaves and the remaining 2 cups stock in a large microwave-safe bowl. Microwave at HIGH until steaming, 3 to 4 minutes. Cover with plastic wrap; let stand 20 minutes. Uncover the mixture, and remove and discard the bay leaves. Add the potato mixture and the remaining ½ teaspoon salt; whisk to combine. Microwave at HIGH until hot, 1 to 2 minutes.

5 Ladle the soup into each of 6 bowls. Drizzle each serving evenly with the cream; sprinkle evenly with the celery leaves and the remaining ¼ teaspoon pepper.

prep pointer

Leeks are tall vegetables with a green top and a white base similar to an oversized green onion. Choose leeks with the most amount of white on their stalks and their roots still intact. To clean, cut off the dark green top and any roots and split the white middle section in half lengthwise. Rinse and chop.

This is one simple condiment that you shouldn't go without. Roasting the bell pepper adds a savory and smoky touch that will jazz up anything from burgers to French fries to a host of sandwiches.

roasted bell pepper sauce

MAKES ½ **CUP**   HANDS-ON TIME: **7 MINUTES**   TOTAL TIME: **20 MINUTES**

1 orange bell pepper
2 teaspoons minced fresh chives
4 tablespoons canola mayonnaise

1 Preheat the broiler.

2 Cut the bell pepper in half lengthwise; discard the seeds and membranes. Place the pepper halves, skin side up, on an aluminum foil–lined baking sheet; flatten each with your hand. Broil 8 minutes or until blackened. Wrap the bell peppers in foil; let stand 5 minutes.

3 Peel and finely chop. Add 4 tablespoons of the chopped bell pepper and the minced chives to the canola mayonnaise; stir until blended.

Romesco, a traditional Catalonian sauce, is essentially comprised of nuts and roasted red pepper and has many uses. Serve it on top of grilled meat, chicken, fish, or even bread. It's a great dipper for crudités and is mild enough to eat on eggs or an omelet for breakfast.

charred red pepper romesco

MAKES **2 CUPS** HANDS-ON TIME: **10 MINUTES** TOTAL TIME: **45 MINUTES**

1 large red bell pepper
1 cup grape tomatoes
6 tablespoons olive oil
1 large shallot, thinly sliced
¼ cup slivered almonds
2 garlic cloves, peeled and crushed
½ ounce baguette, torn into small pieces
2 teaspoons red wine vinegar
½ teaspoon table salt
½ teaspoon smoked paprika
½ teaspoon freshly ground black pepper

1 Preheat the oven to 425°F.

2 Cut the bell pepper in half lengthwise; remove and discard the seeds and ribs. Place the bell pepper halves and tomatoes on a half-sized baking sheet; add 2 tablespoons of the oil, and toss to coat. Turn the bell pepper halves cut sides down. Bake at 425°F until the vegetables are beginning to blacken, about 20 minutes.

3 Remove the vegetables from the oven. Add the shallots, almonds, and garlic; stir to combine. Return to the oven, and bake until the shallots and garlic are tender and golden, 15 to 20 minutes. (Be careful not to burn the garlic. Stir the mixture if any almonds or garlic look like they are burning.)

4 Scrape the vegetable mixture and any accumulated pan juices into a food processor. Add the baguette pieces, vinegar, salt, paprika, black pepper, and remaining ¼ cup oil; process until almost smooth, 30 seconds to 1 minute.

prep pointer

We call for slivered almonds here, but you can use whole almonds as well. For other options, use walnuts, pine nuts, or even sunflower seeds.

Remove the husks from the tomatillos and rinse off the fruit to remove the sticky layer. If you want to speed this up a little bit, you can chop the vegetables in the food processor. It's easy enough to double or triple the recipe to make it for a crowd.

blackened tomatillo salsa

MAKES **2 CUPS**   HANDS-ON TIME: **10 MINUTES**   TOTAL TIME: **32 MINUTES**

1 poblano chile
1 pound tomatillos (about 8 medium tomatillos), husks removed, cored
½ cup chopped white onion (about 1 small onion)
½ cup packed fresh cilantro leaves
¼ cup extra-virgin olive oil
2 garlic cloves, peeled
1 teaspoon ground cumin
¾ teaspoon table salt

1 Preheat the broiler with the oven rack 8 inches from the heat.

2 Cut the poblano in half lengthwise; remove and discard the seeds and ribs. Place the poblano halves, cut sides down, and the tomatillos on a half-sized baking sheet coated with cooking spray. Broil until the skins are blackened and the vegetables are soft, 12 to 15 minutes. Cool 10 minutes.

3 Cut the poblano halves and tomatillos into bite-sized pieces, and place in a medium bowl. Add the onion, cilantro, oil, garlic, cumin, and salt; stir to combine.

flavor note

Charring the tomatillos and poblano is a great way to add flavor to the salsa without adding more ingredients. Seeding and de-ribbing the poblano keeps the salsa from being too hot, as most of the pepper's heat is stored in these regions.

This pesto has a slightly richer garlic flavor than other pestos. It is a fantastic spread for toasted baguettes or sauce for noodles.

roasted garlic pesto

MAKES ABOUT **1¼ CUPS**   HANDS-ON TIME: **10 MINUTES**   TOTAL TIME: **55 MINUTES**

6 garlic cloves, peeled
1 cup plus 1 tablespoon extra-virgin olive oil
⅓ cup pine nuts
4 cups packed fresh basil leaves
2 ounces Parmesan cheese, grated (about ½ cup)
2 ounces Romano cheese, grated (about ½ cup)
½ teaspoon table salt
½ teaspoon freshly ground black pepper

1 Preheat oven to 425°F.

2 Place the garlic cloves on a square of aluminum foil. Drizzle with 1 tablespoon of the oil, and wrap the foil around the garlic. Place the foil packet on a quarter-sized baking sheet. Bake at 425°F until tender, about 35 minutes.

3 Place the pine nuts next to the foil packet on the baking sheet. Bake until the pine nuts are lightly toasted, 2 to 3 minutes. Unwrap the foil packet; let stand until the garlic is cool enough to handle, about 10 minutes.

4 Place the roasted garlic, pine nuts, basil, cheeses, salt, pepper, and ¼ cup of the oil in a food processor; process until finely ground, about 30 seconds. With the processor running, slowly drizzle in the remaining ¾ cup oil through the food chute, and process until smooth and incorporated, 30 seconds to 1 minute.

prep pointer

Because 4 ounces of the store-packaged variety can be expensive, purchase basil in bulk or harvest it from a garden. Blanching, shocking, and storing it in the refrigerator will keep the basil green for days.

You can find tahini in supermarkets or in Middle Eastern food stores.

roasted vegetable dip

MAKES **2¼ CUPS**   HANDS-ON TIME: **8 MINUTES**   TOTAL TIME: **43 MINUTES**

1 pound carrots, peeled and cut into ½-inch slices
1 large Vidalia or other sweet onion, cut into
   6 wedges
1 red bell pepper, cut into 1-inch pieces
1 tablespoon olive oil
2 tablespoons chili sauce with garlic
¼ cup tahini (roasted sesame seed paste)
¼ teaspoon table salt
¼ teaspoon freshly ground black pepper
Chopped fresh flat-leaf parsley (optional)
9 sesame breadsticks

1 Preheat the oven to 450°F.

2 Combine the carrots, onion wedges, bell pepper, and olive oil in a large bowl, and toss well. Place the vegetables on a baking sheet. Bake at 450°F until tender, stirring every 15 minutes, 35 minutes.

3 Place the roasted vegetables, chili sauce, tahini, salt, and pepper in a food processor; process until smooth. Garnish with the chopped parsley, if desired. Serve with the breadsticks.

Caramelized sweet shallots and silky mascarpone cheese add new-school touches to onion-soup dip. No need to waste time peeling all the shallots; after roasting, the papery skins easily slip away. If you're topping the dip with bacon, see our Prep Pointer for cooking it in the oven (page 29) or use leftover cooked bacon.

roasted shallot dip

MAKES ABOUT **4 CUPS**   HANDS-ON TIME: **20 MINUTES**   TOTAL TIME: **5 HOURS, 35 MINUTES, INCLUDES CHILLING**

1½ pounds shallots, unpeeled and root ends trimmed

3 unpeeled garlic cloves

2 tablespoons olive oil

¾ teaspoon kosher salt, plus more for seasoning

½ teaspoon freshly ground black pepper, plus more for seasoning

1 (8-ounce) container sour cream

1 (8-ounce) container mascarpone cheese

⅓ cup thinly sliced fresh chives

1 tablespoon fresh lemon juice

2 teaspoons whole-grain Dijon mustard

Dash of hot sauce

Cooked and crumbled bacon, grated lemon rind, chopped fresh chives (optional)

1 Preheat the oven to 425°F.

2 Cut the shallots in half. Toss together the shallots, garlic, and oil on a baking sheet; sprinkle with ¾ teaspoon of the salt and ½ teaspoon of the pepper. Bake at 425°F until the shallots are light brown and the skins are charred, stirring twice, 45 to 50 minutes. Cool completely on the baking sheet on a wire rack, about 30 minutes. Remove and discard the papery skins from the shallots and garlic, and coarsely chop the shallots and garlic.

3 Stir together the sour cream, mascarpone, chives, lemon juice, Dijon mustard, and hot sauce; fold in the shallot mixture. Add salt and pepper to taste. Cover and chill 4 to 48 hours. Stir before serving. Add more salt and pepper to taste just before serving, if desired. Garnish with the bacon, lemon rind, and chives, if desired.

prep pointer

Prepare this recipe up to 2 days in advance; chill in an airtight container. Let stand at room temperature 30 minutes before serving.

Try a unique twist on classic hummus by using cauliflower florets as the key ingredient. Before serving, top the hummus with 1 tablespoon cauliflower and olives for a beautiful presentation. (Also pictured on page 200)

cauliflower hummus WITH green olives

MAKES 1½ **CUPS**   HANDS-ON TIME: **10 MINUTES**   TOTAL TIME: **30 MINUTES**

1 cup cauliflower florets
2 teaspoons olive oil
¾ teaspoon curry powder
¼ teaspoon kosher salt
¼ teaspoon freshly ground black pepper

EASY HUMMUS:
2 tablespoons tahini (roasted sesame seed paste)
2 tablespoons fresh lemon juice
1 tablespoon extra-virgin olive oil
1 (15-ounce) can unsalted chickpeas (garbanzo beans), rinsed and drained
¼ teaspoon kosher salt
3 tablespoons water
1 garlic clove

2 tablespoons chopped pitted Castelvetrano olives

1 Preheat the oven to 450°F.

2 Toss together the cauliflower florets, olive oil, curry powder, salt, and black pepper. Spread in an even layer on a baking sheet. Bake at 450°F until tender, stirring after 10 minutes, 20 minutes. Cool 10 minutes.

3 Meanwhile, make the Easy Hummus: Place the tahini, lemon juice, olive oil, chickpeas, salt, water, and garlic clove in the bowl of a food processor; process until smooth.

4 Reserve 1 tablespoon of the cooled cauliflower. Add the remaining cooled cauliflower to the food processor with the Easy Hummus; process until smooth. Top the hummus with the reserved 1 tablespoon cauliflower and the olives.

The beet flavor (if not the color) in this dip is very subtle, with a nutty edge from walnuts and walnut oil. Pair with crunchy crudités.

roasted beet hummus

MAKES **ABOUT 2 CUPS**   HANDS-ON TIME: **15 MINUTES**   TOTAL TIME: **1 HOUR, 17 MINUTES**

1 small red beet
¼ cup coarsely chopped walnuts
4 garlic cloves, peeled and halved
1 teaspoon grated lemon rind
¼ cup water
2 tablespoons fresh lemon juice
2 tablespoons walnut oil
¾ teaspoon freshly ground black pepper
½ teaspoon kosher salt
1 (15-ounce) can chickpeas (garbanzo beans), rinsed
    and drained

1 Preheat the oven to 450°F.

2 Leave the root and 1-inch stem on the beet; scrub the beet with a brush. Wrap the beet in aluminum foil. Place on a baking sheet. Bake at 450°F for 35 minutes. Add the walnuts and garlic to the baking sheet. Bake until the nuts are toasted, 7 minutes. Cool 10 minutes. Trim off the beet root; rub off the skin. Cut the beet into quarters.

3 Place the garlic in a food processor; process until finely chopped. Add the beet; process until very finely chopped. Add the walnuts, lemon rind, water, lemon juice, oil, black pepper, salt, and chickpeas. Process until smooth.

flavor note

Top the hummus with crumbled blue cheese, chopped toasted walnuts, and microgreens to amp up the flavor.

Stirring in the reserved chickpea liquid reinforces the chickpea flavor and makes this hummus creamy, delicious, and smooth. It can be used as a dipper or as a spread.

toasted chickpea hummus

MAKES **2 CUPS**   HANDS-ON TIME: **10 MINUTES**   TOTAL TIME: **32 MINUTES**

1 (14½-ounce) can chickpeas (garbanzo beans)
3 unpeeled garlic cloves
5 tablespoons olive oil
3 tablespoons pine nuts
2 tablespoons tahini (roasted sesame seed paste)
2 tablespoons fresh lemon juice
½ teaspoon kosher salt
⅛ teaspoon crushed red pepper, plus more for topping

1 Preheat the oven to 375°F.

2 Drain the chickpeas, reserving the chickpea liquid. Place the chickpeas and garlic cloves on a jelly-roll pan. Add 2 tablespoons of the oil; toss to coat. Bake at 375°F until browned, stirring after 15 minutes, 20 to 25 minutes. Arrange the pine nuts in a single layer in 1 corner of the pan; bake until the pine nuts are golden, 2 to 3 minutes. Set aside 1 tablespoon of the toasted pine nuts.

3 Squeeze the garlic from the cloves into a food processor; discard the skins. Place the toasted chickpeas, tahini, lemon juice, salt, ⅛ teaspoon of the red pepper, and remaining 3 tablespoons oil and 2 tablespoons toasted pine nuts in the food processor. Process until smooth, about 1 minute. Stir in the reserved chickpea liquid. Scoop the mixture into a serving bowl; top with the reserved 1 tablespoon toasted pine nuts and additional crushed red pepper.

prep pointer

If you have a choice, buy packaged tahini in the wider container rather than the deeper container. Eventually the bottom of the tahini starts to harden, and it will be easier to stir in a shallower container.

desserts

Spread the batter as evenly as possible on the baking sheet. When shaping the shells, allow plenty of room so you can work quickly.

chocolate tacos WITH ice cream AND peanuts

SERVES **8**   HANDS-ON TIME: **40 MINUTES**   TOTAL TIME: **1 HOUR, 22 MINUTES**

½ cup powdered sugar
1.1 ounces all-purpose flour (about ¼ cup)
3 tablespoons unsweetened cocoa
1 teaspoon cornstarch
¼ teaspoon table salt
3 tablespoons egg whites (from 2 eggs)
1 teaspoon milk
¼ teaspoon vanilla extract
½ cup semisweet chocolate chips
1 teaspoon canola oil
½ cup unsalted dry-roasted peanuts, finely chopped
2⅔ cups vanilla ice cream

1 Preheat the oven to 400°F.

2 Combine the sugar, flour, cocoa, cornstarch, and salt in a large bowl, stirring well. Stir in the egg whites, milk, and vanilla.

3 Coat a baking sheet with cooking spray. Using your finger, draw 4 (5-inch) circles on the baking sheet. Spoon 1 tablespoon of the batter onto each circle, spreading to the edges of the circle using the back of a spoon. Bake at 400°F until the edges begin to brown, 6 minutes.

Loosen the edges with a spatula; remove from the baking sheet.

4 Balance 4 wooden spoons between objects that are about 6 inches apart. Working quickly, gently drape each taco over the suspended wooden spoons, gently shaping into a shell; cool completely. (The shells are delicate and should be handled carefully when shaped.) Repeat the procedure to form a total of 8 shells.

5 Combine the chocolate chips and oil in a microwave-safe bowl. Microwave at HIGH 1 minute or until the chocolate melts, stirring after 30 seconds; stir until smooth. Gently spread about 1 teaspoon of the chocolate mixture on the top third of the outside of both sides of the cooled shells, and sprinkle with about 1 teaspoon of the chopped peanuts. Spoon ⅓ cup of the ice cream into each shell. Drizzle the remaining chocolate mixture evenly over the ice cream; sprinkle with the remaining peanuts. Freeze for at least 30 minutes before serving.

desserts

Dulce de leche is the star in these bite-sized treats. Look for it in the baking aisle or in the international foods section.

caramel-chocolate tartlets

SERVES **30**   HANDS-ON TIME: **15 MINUTES**   TOTAL TIME: **16 MINUTES**

2 (1.9-ounce) packages frozen mini phyllo shells (30 shells), thawed

1 (13.4-ounce) can dulce de leche (caramelized sweetened condensed milk)

1 cup semisweet chocolate chips

⅓ cup salted dry-roasted peanuts, chopped

1 Place the phyllo shells on a baking sheet. Spoon 1 heaping teaspoon of the dulce de leche into each shell. Place the chocolate morsels in a small microwave-safe bowl; microwave, uncovered, at HIGH about 1 minute, stirring once, until smooth. Spoon 1 teaspoon of the melted chocolate over the dulce de leche in each shell.

2 Sprinkle the tartlets evenly with the peanuts. Freeze 1 minute to set the chocolate. Store, covered, in the refrigerator.

prep pointer

To make ahead, freeze the tartlets in the trays they come in and store in zip-top plastic freezer bags. Remove from the freezer 1 hour before serving.

Sheets of crisp, paper-thin phyllo dough encase a filling of toasted ground almonds, with red-skinned pears as the crowning touch. We call for Anjou, but you can also use Bartlett, Bosc, or Concorde pears.

frangipane pear tarts

SERVES **6**   HANDS-ON TIME: **40 MINUTES**   TOTAL TIME: **1 HOUR, 3 MINUTES**

⅔ cup blanched whole almonds, toasted
½ cup sugar
2 tablespoons butter
¾ teaspoon vanilla extract
⅛ teaspoon table salt
1 large egg
12 sheets frozen phyllo dough, thawed
Cooking spray
2 red Anjou pears, cored and thinly sliced
2 tablespoons apple jelly
Sliced almonds and mint leaves (optional)

1 Preheat the oven to 375°F.

2 Place the almonds and sugar in a food processor; process until very finely ground. Add 1½ teaspoons of the butter, vanilla, salt, and egg; process to form a sticky paste.

3 Place the remaining 1½ tablespoons butter in a small microwave-safe bowl; microwave at HIGH 20 seconds or until the butter melts. Arrange 1 phyllo sheet on a cutting board or other work surface (cover the remaining phyllo to prevent drying); brush lightly with the butter. Top with another phyllo sheet; brush lightly with the butter. Fold the phyllo stack in half lengthwise to form a 9- x 7-inch stack. Loosely fold the edges of the phyllo up toward the center to create a 4½-inch rimmed tart shell. Place on a baking sheet lined with parchment paper; coat the phyllo shell with cooking spray. Repeat the procedure with the remaining phyllo sheets, butter, and cooking spray to form 6 shells.

4 Spread about 2 tablespoons of the almond mixture over each tart shell; top each with about 6 slightly overlapping pear slices. Bake at 375°F until the phyllo is browned and crisp, about 23 minutes.

5 Place the jelly in a small microwave-safe bowl; microwave at HIGH for 20 seconds or until the jelly melts. Brush the jelly evenly over the tarts. Sprinkle with the sliced almonds and mint leaves, if desired.

Even if you're a baking newbie, you can turn these out with ease, thanks to frozen puff pastry. To keep the pastries from sticking to the parchment paper, remove them right after baking. (Also pictured on page 224)

boysenberry danishes

SERVES **9**   HANDS-ON TIME: **30 MINUTES**   TOTAL TIME: **1 HOUR**

6 ounces cream cheese, softened

3 tablespoons wildflower or other mild honey

1½ tablespoons cornstarch (1 tablespoon if using raspberries and blackberries)

¼ cup sugar

1 large egg

3 teaspoons water

1 sheet frozen puff pastry dough, thawed

2 cups boysenberries or 1 cup each raspberries and blackberries

1 Preheat the oven to 375°F.

2 Place the cheese and honey in a food processor; whirl until blended, scraping down the inside of the bowl as needed.

3 Combine the cornstarch and sugar in a medium bowl. Whisk together the egg and 2 teaspoons of the water in another bowl until blended. Set the bowls aside.

4 Roll the puff pastry into a 12-inch square on a lightly floured work surface. Cut into 9 squares, each 4 inches. Transfer to a baking sheet lined with parchment paper. Gently spread about 1½ tablespoons of the cheese mixture in a 3-inch-long diagonal on each square.

5 Gently stir the berries and the remaining 1 teaspoon water into the cornstarch mixture. Continue stirring gently until the dry cornstarch disappears, 2 to 3 minutes. Spoon the mixture over the cheese.

6 For each danish, pull a corner over the filling almost to the other side of it and brush the top of the dough with the egg wash. Fold the opposite corner over the first one and press to seal. Leave the remaining corners flat. Brush the dough all over with the egg wash.

7 Bake the danishes at 375°F until deep golden and crisp, 30 to 35 minutes. Transfer to cooling racks and serve warm or cool.

flavor note

Boysenberries are simply a hybrid between blackberries and raspberries and were first created by their namesake, Charles Boysen. They are slightly more tart than either of their root berries.

This perfect blend of a pie and a crumble makes use of summer's best fruits. Serve it after dinner or Sunday lunch with a cup of coffee and a scoop of vanilla ice cream.

peach AND plum crostada

SERVES **8**   HANDS-ON TIME: **30 MINUTES**   TOTAL TIME: **2 HOUR, 30 MINUTES**

2 ripe, firm peaches, peeled, pitted, and thinly sliced

3 small plums or 1 medium-sized ripe, firm plum, pitted and thinly sliced

¼ cup plus 1 tablespoon sugar

1½ teaspoons finely grated lemon rind

2 tablespoons all-purpose flour

⅛ teaspoon table salt

4 tablespoons cold unsalted butter, cut into small pieces

¼ cup finely chopped pecans

1 sheet frozen puff pastry dough, thawed

1 large egg

¼ teaspoon cold water

1 Toss the fruit and 1 tablespoon of the sugar in a small bowl. Let stand for 20 minutes.

2 Preheat the oven to 450°F. Set a rack in the lower-middle position.

3 Line a baking sheet with parchment paper.

4 Make the topping: Combine the remaining ¼ cup sugar and lemon rind in a bowl. Stir in the flour and salt. Cut in the butter using a pastry blender or 2 knives until the mixture is crumbly. Toss in the pecans.

5 Roll out the puff pastry to a rough 14-inch round on a well-floured surface. Carefully transfer to the prepared baking sheet. Strain the fruit mixture; discard the juice. Spoon evenly onto the pastry, leaving a 2-inch border. Sprinkle the topping over the filling; fold over the edges of the pastry. Whisk the egg with the cold water and lightly brush the edges of the pastry with the egg wash. Refrigerate for 20 minutes.

6 Bake at 450°F until the pastry begins to brown, about 20 minutes. Lower the heat to 400°F; bake until the crust is deep golden brown, the bottom is cooked through, and the filling is bubbling, about 20 more minutes. Cover with aluminum foil if the crust is browning too quickly.

7 Let the crostada rest on the baking sheet for 10 minutes. Transfer to a wire rack to cool completely, about 30 minutes. Cut into wedges and serve at room temperature.

Making personal galettes for each dinner guest means no one is fighting over that last bite! Toasted almonds sprinkled over the dough provide a bit of crunch and subtle nutty flavor to these adorable pastries. For a fancy presentation, serve with whipped cream.

individual apricot galettes

SERVES **8** HANDS-ON TIME: **7 MINUTES** TOTAL TIME: **27 MINUTES**

1 (14.1-ounce) package refrigerated pie dough
3 tablespoons sliced almonds, toasted
8 apricots, thinly sliced
1 tablespoon sugar
2 tablespoons apricot preserves
Fresh thyme leaves (optional)

1 Preheat the oven to 425°F.

2 Roll 1 dough piece onto a lightly floured surface. Cut 4 (4¾-inch) rounds from the dough, rerolling the scraps as needed. Place the rounds 1 inch apart on baking sheets lined with parchment paper. Repeat with the remaining dough piece. Discard the remaining dough.

3 Sprinkle about 1 teaspoon of the almonds over the center of each dough round. Combine the apricot slices and sugar in a bowl; toss to coat. Arrange the apricot slices in an even layer over each dough round, leaving a ¾-inch border around the edges. Fold the dough border over the apricots, pressing gently to seal (the dough will only partially cover the apricots).

4 Place the preserves in a small microwave-safe bowl. Microwave at HIGH 10 seconds or until soft. Brush the dough and apricot slices with the preserves. Bake at 425°F until golden brown, 20 to 23 minutes. Sprinkle with the thyme leaves, if desired, and serve warm.

You can substitute 1 teaspoon of cinnamon and nutmeg for the cardamom. (Also pictured on page 225)

spiced peach galette

SERVES **8 TO 10**   HANDS-ON TIME: **45 MINUTES**   TOTAL TIME: **4 HOURS, 5 MINUTES, INCLUDES CHILLING**

CRUST:

11¾ ounces all-purpose flour (about 2¾ cups)

2 tablespoons granulated sugar

1 teaspoon kosher salt

12 tablespoons cold butter (1½ sticks), cubed

¼ cup frozen shortening, cubed

8 to 10 tablespoons ice water

FILLING:

½ cup granulated sugar

2 teaspoons ground cardamom

1 tablespoon cornstarch

6 medium-sized ripe, firm peaches

1 teaspoon fresh lemon juice

1 teaspoon vanilla extract

1 tablespoon grated fresh ginger

2 tablespoons heavy cream

1 tablespoon turbinado sugar (optional)

1 Make the Crust: Place the flour, sugar, and salt in the large bowl of a food processor; pulse 5 times to combine. Add the butter and shortening. Pulse 12 to 15 times until the mixture resembles small peas. Evenly sprinkle 8 tablespoons of the ice water over the top of the flour and butter mixture. Pulse 5 times to combine. Pinch the dough; if it does not stick together, add up to 2 tablespoons ice water, 1 tablespoon at a time, pulsing 3 to 5 times to combine after each addition. Turn the dough out onto a work surface, and knead 4 to 5 times to

bring together. Shape into a 1-inch-thick oval. Wrap with plastic wrap, and chill 1 to 24 hours.

2 Preheat the oven to 425°F.

3 Let the dough stand at room temperature 15 minutes. Place on a lightly floured sheet of parchment paper, and roll into a 12- x 16-inch oval about ⅛ inch thick. Transfer the dough and parchment to a baking sheet; chill until ready to use.

4 Make the Filling: Stir together the sugar, cardamom, and cornstarch in a large bowl. Cut each peach into 8 wedges, and add to the sugar mixture. Gently toss to coat. Add the lemon juice, vanilla, and ginger; gently toss to combine.

5 Remove the peaches from the bowl, reserving 4 tablespoons of the liquid. Arrange the peaches in a single layer on the dough, overlapping slightly, leaving a 1 ½-inch border along each edge. Cut the pastry border every 4 inches, and fold each piece up over the fruit. Brush the crust with the heavy cream, and, if desired, sprinkle with turbinado sugar. Drizzle the reserved 4 tablespoons liquid over the peaches.

6 Bake at 425°F for 15 minutes. Reduce the heat to 350°F, and bake until golden brown, about 40 minutes. Cool 10 minutes on baking sheet; transfer to a wire rack, and cool 1 hour.

Make the dough ahead and refrigerate or freeze (just remember to thaw completely before rolling). You can sub the scraped seeds from one vanilla bean pod or 1 teaspoon vanilla extract for the vanilla bean paste.

apple galette WITH vanilla yogurt drizzle

SERVES **8**   HANDS-ON TIME: **31 MINUTES**   TOTAL TIME: **3 HOURS, 26 MINUTES, INCLUDES CHILLING**

4 ounces all-purpose flour (about ¾ cup plus 2 tablespoons)

3.1 ounces whole-wheat flour (about ⅔ cup)

1 tablespoon granulated sugar

1 teaspoon kosher salt

5½ tablespoons chilled unsalted butter, cut into ½-inch pieces

3 tablespoons whole milk

¾ cup plain yogurt

¼ cup packed light brown sugar

2 tablespoons fresh lemon juice

2 teaspoons vanilla extract

½ teaspoon ground cinnamon

⅛ teaspoon ground nutmeg

⅛ teaspoon ground ginger

2 pounds Cortland or Fuji apples, cut crosswise into ⅛-inch-thick slices

1 large egg white, lightly beaten

2 teaspoons vanilla bean paste

1 Weigh or lightly spoon ¾ cup of the all-purpose flour and the whole-wheat flour into dry measuring cups; level with a knife. Place the flours, granulated sugar, and ½ teaspoon of the salt in the bowl of a food processor; pulse 3 to 4 times to combine. Add the butter; pulse 8 to 10 times or until the mixture resembles a coarse meal. Add the milk and ¼ cup of the yogurt; pulse 20 times or until pea-sized lumps form and the dough begins to pull away from the sides of the bowl. Turn the dough out onto a lightly floured work surface; shape into a 6-inch disk. Cover with plastic wrap, and chill 2 hours or overnight.

2 Preheat the oven to 425°F.

3 Combine the remaining 2 tablespoons all-purpose flour, ¼ teaspoon of the salt, brown sugar, lemon juice, vanilla, cinnamon, nutmeg, ginger, and apples in a large bowl; toss to coat.

4 Unwrap the dough; place on a large piece of lightly floured parchment paper. Roll the dough to a 15-inch circle. Place the parchment paper with the dough on a baking sheet. Spoon the apple mixture onto the dough, leaving a 2-inch border. Fold the edges of the dough over the filling to partially cover. Brush the edges of the dough with the egg white. Bake at 425°F until the crust is golden brown, 25 minutes. Let stand at room temperature 30 minutes. Cut into 8 wedges.

5 Combine the remaining ¼ teaspoon salt, remaining ½ cup yogurt, and vanilla bean paste in a bowl, stirring with a whisk. Drizzle the yogurt mixture over the galette.

desserts

239

You'll love this airy roulade's light and creamy lemon filling.

lemon–poppy seed roulade

SERVES **10** HANDS-ON TIME: **35 MINUTES** TOTAL TIME: **3 HOURS, 18 MINUTES, INCLUDES CHILLING**

½ cup granulated sugar

6 large eggs, separated

2 tablespoons poppy seeds

1 teaspoon vanilla extract

2 tablespoons lemon zest, plus 4 teaspoons fresh
  juice, plus additional zest for garnish

¾ cup cake flour (about 2 ⅞ ounces)

1¼ teaspoons baking powder

⅜ teaspoon table salt

2 cups (about 8 ounces) powdered sugar

8 ounces cream cheese, softened

¼ cup unsalted butter, softened

½ cup heavy cream, chilled

1 Preheat the oven to 375°F. Line a jelly-roll pan with lightly greased parchment paper.

2 Beat the granulated sugar and egg yolks with a heavy-duty electric stand mixer on medium-high speed until thick and pale, about 4 minutes. Stir in the poppy seeds, vanilla, 1 tablespoon of the lemon zest, and 1 teaspoon of the lemon juice.

3 Beat the egg whites in a separate bowl on medium-high speed until soft peaks form, 1 to 2 minutes. Stir one-fourth of the egg whites into the granulated sugar mixture. Gently fold in the remaining egg whites. Sift the cake flour, baking powder, and ¼ teaspoon of the salt over the egg mixture; gently fold just until incorporated. Spread the mixture in the prepared pan. Bake at 375°F until the cake springs back when touched, about 8 minutes. Cool in the pan on a wire rack 5 minutes.

4 Sprinkle 3 tablespoons of the powdered sugar over the cake. Run a knife along the sides of the cake; invert onto a parchment paper-lined work surface. Peel off the top layer of the parchment from the cake; discard the parchment. Sprinkle 3 tablespoons of the powdered sugar evenly over the cake. Starting at 1 short side, carefully roll cake and bottom layer of the parchment together. Transfer to a wire rack, seam side down, and cool completely, about 30 minutes.

5 Beat the cream cheese and butter on medium speed until smooth, about 4 minutes. Gradually add 1½ cups of the powdered sugar and the remaining 1 tablespoon each lemon zest and lemon juice, and ⅛ teaspoon salt; beat until smooth, about 2 minutes. Beat the heavy cream in a separate bowl on medium-high speed until peaks form, 1 to 2 minutes; fold into the cream cheese mixture.

6 Carefully unroll the cake. Spread the cream cheese mixture over the cake, leaving a ½-inch border. Starting at 1 short side, reroll the cake without the parchment. Place the cake, seam side down, on a serving platter. Cover and chill 2 hours.

7 Sprinkle the cake with the remaining 2 tablespoons powdered sugar; garnish with the lemon zest.

This sweet and summery dessert is perfect for a crowd. Serve it with a scoop of vanilla ice cream. You can also use cream cheese frosting instead of vanilla, if you prefer.

fresh strawberry sheet cake

SERVES **16**   HANDS-ON TIME: **20 MINUTES**   TOTAL TIME: **1 HOUR, 50 MINUTES**

20 tablespoons (2½ sticks) unsalted butter, softened
2½ cups sugar
5 large eggs
1 tablespoon fresh lemon juice
1½ teaspoons vanilla extract
12¾ ounces all-purpose flour (about 3 cups)
1 (3-ounce) package strawberry-flavored gelatin
1 teaspoon baking soda
1 teaspoon table salt
1¼ cups buttermilk
1 cup chopped fresh strawberries
2 (12-ounce) containers ready-to-spread vanilla frosting (such as Betty Crocker)
Whole fresh strawberries (optional)

1 Preheat the oven to 350°F.

2 Line a half-sized baking sheet with parchment paper; lightly grease the parchment with cooking spray.

3 Beat the butter in a large bowl with an electric mixer on medium speed until creamy. With the mixer running, gradually add the sugar, and beat until fluffy, about 3 minutes. Add the eggs, 1 at a time, beating until well combined after each addition. Beat in the lemon juice and vanilla.

4 Weigh or lightly spoon the flour into dry measuring cups; level with a knife. Stir together the flour, gelatin, baking soda, and salt in a separate bowl. Add the flour mixture and buttermilk alternately to the butter mixture in 5 additions, beginning and ending with the flour mixture, beating on low speed just until blended after each addition. Stir in the chopped strawberries. Spread the mixture on the prepared baking sheet. Bake at 350°F until a wooden pick inserted in the center comes out clean, about 30 minutes.

5 Cool the cake completely on the baking sheet on a wire rack, about 1 hour. Spread the cooled cake with the frosting. Garnish with the whole strawberries, if desired.

flavor note

Use ripe summer strawberries for the best flavor. Chop the strawberries just before stirring them into the cake batter to prevent additional liquid (juice from the berries) from being added.

You've heard of breakfast for dinner—why not brunch for dessert? Adding cinnamon and caramelized apples to this classic, eggy pancake dish takes breakfast to dessert in no time.

cinnamon-apple dutch baby

SERVES **12**   HANDS-ON TIME: **25 MINUTES**   TOTAL TIME: **55 MINUTES**

2 medium-sized Golden Delicious apples, thinly sliced

1 tablespoon canola oil

1 teaspoon ground cinnamon

½ teaspoon table salt

1½ cups whole milk

6 large eggs

2 teaspoons vanilla extract

6⅜ ounces all-purpose flour (about 1½ cups)

¼ cup granulated sugar

8 tablespoons unsalted butter (1 stick), melted

¼ cup powdered sugar (optional)

1 Preheat the oven to 425°F.

2 Combine the apples, oil, cinnamon, and ¼ teaspoon of the salt on a half-sized baking sheet; toss to coat. Bake at 425°F until the apples are tender and beginning to brown, stirring after 10 minutes, 15 to 20 minutes.

3 Place the milk, eggs, vanilla, and remaining ¼ teaspoon salt in a blender; process until smooth, about 30 seconds. Whisk together the flour and granulated sugar in a large bowl. Add the flour mixture to the milk mixture in 3 additions; process until smooth after each addition.

4 Drizzle the melted butter over the apple mixture; stir to combine. (Make sure the butter completely coats the bottom of the baking sheet.) Pour the batter evenly over the apple mixture. Bake at 425°F until puffy and golden, 15 to 20 minutes.

5 Sprinkle evenly with the powdered sugar, if desired. Cut into squares; serve immediately.

prep pointer

If your oven has racks on smooth-rolling casters, pull the rack out to pour the butter and batter onto the baking sheet while it is still on the rack to help prevent spills.

Mississippi Mud Cake is a classic sheet cake filled with marshmallows and chopped pecans and covered in a rich chocolate frosting. (Also pictured on page 224)

mississippi mud cake

SERVES **15**   HANDS-ON TIME: **20 MINUTES**   TOTAL TIME: **56 MINUTES**

1 cup chopped pecans, toasted
16 tablespoons (2 sticks) butter
4 ounces semisweet chocolate, chopped
2 cups granulated sugar
6½ ounces all-purpose flour (about 1½ cups)
½ cup unsweetened cocoa
4 large eggs
1 teaspoon vanilla extract
¾ teaspoon table salt
1 (10.5-ounce) bag miniature marshmallows

CHOCOLATE FROSTING:
8 tablespoons (1 stick) butter
⅓ cup unsweetened cocoa
⅓ cup milk
1 (16-ounce) package powdered sugar
1 teaspoon vanilla extract

1 Preheat the oven to 350°F.

2 Place the pecans in a single layer on a baking sheet. Bake at 350°F until toasted, 8 to 10 minutes.

3 Place 1 cup butter and the semisweet chocolate in a large microwave-safe glass bowl; microwave at HIGH 1 minute or until melted and smooth, stirring every 30 seconds.

4 Whisk the sugar, flour, cocoa, eggs, vanilla, and salt into the chocolate mixture. Pour the batter onto a greased jelly-roll pan.

5 Bake at 350°F for 20 minutes. Remove from the oven, and sprinkle evenly with miniature marshmallows. Bake until golden brown, 8 to 10 more minutes.

6 Meanwhile, make the Chocolate Frosting: Place the butter in a large cleaned and dried microwave-safe glass bowl; microwave at HIGH until melted, about 30 seconds. Add the cocoa and the milk to the butter; mix well until combined and slightly thickened. Beat in the powdered sugar and vanilla at medium-high speed with an electric mixer until smooth.

7 Drizzle the warm cake with the Chocolate Frosting; sprinkle with the toasted pecans.

This salty-sweet treat gets a satisfying crunch from the peanuts and pretzels that balance the creamy, melted chocolate.

marbled peanut AND pretzel bark

SERVES **10**   HANDS-ON TIME: **15 MINUTES**   TOTAL TIME: **55 MINUTES, INCLUDES CHILLING**

1 (8-ounce) semisweet chocolate baking bar, finely chopped

½ (8-ounce) white chocolate baking bar, finely chopped

½ cup roughly chopped roasted salted peanuts

½ cup broken pretzels

1 Preheat the oven to 200°F.

2 Line a quarter-sized baking sheet with parchment paper, letting the parchment extend 2 inches past the long sides.

3 Spread the chopped semisweet chocolate in an even layer on the prepared baking sheet. Sprinkle the chopped white chocolate evenly over the semisweet chocolate. Turn off the oven. Place the baking sheet in the oven; bake until the chocolate melts, about 10 minutes.

4 Remove the baking sheet from the oven, and swirl the mixture with a wooden spoon or the tip of a knife (the thinner the instrument the more defined the lines) to create a marbled surface. Sprinkle the peanuts and the pretzels evenly over the melted chocolate. Chill until solid, about 30 minutes, or let stand at room temperature until solid, about 1 hour.

5 Using the excess parchment as handles, remove the bark from the baking sheet. Break the bark into bite-sized pieces.

prep pointer

Buy the best-quality chocolate your store carries. The pay-off is significant. Using baking chocolate ensures an even melt, as chips will retain their shape.

This is a convenient go-to last-minute dessert. Leave the mixer in the cabinet—you can mix up this dough with a spoon.

pb & chocolate pan cookie

MAKES **ABOUT 24 PIECES**   HANDS-ON TIME: **10 MINUTES**   TOTAL TIME: **35 MINUTES**

¾ cup chunky peanut butter
2 large eggs
1 teaspoon vanilla extract
1 cup firmly packed light brown sugar
2 cups baking mix
1 (12-ounce) package dark chocolate chips

1 Preheat the oven to 325°F.

2 Stir together the peanut butter, eggs, and vanilla in a large bowl.

3 Stir in the brown sugar until combined. Add the baking mix and ¾ cup of the dark chocolate chips, stirring just until moistened. Spread the mixture on a lightly greased jelly-roll pan.

4 Bake at 325°F until golden brown, 20 minutes. Remove from the oven, and sprinkle evenly with the remaining 1¼ cups dark chocolate chips; let stand until the chocolate melts, about 5 minutes. Spread the melted chocolate evenly over the top. Cut into pieces.

prep pointer

Be careful not to overcook the dough so the cookie doesn't dry out.

The secrets to this fantastic shortbread are rice flour for the sandy texture and a slow-and-low baking process to develop the flavor. It's a recipe that lends itself to easy, festive riffing (think sprinkles and snowflakes), and one you'll be glad to have in your repertoire for years.

scottish shortbread

MAKES **68 (1- X 3-INCH) BARS** OR **48 (2-INCH) SQUARES**   HANDS-ON TIME: **40 MINUTES**
TOTAL TIME: **2 HOURS, 50 MINUTES, INCLUDES OPTIONAL BAKE TIME**

40 tablespoons (5 sticks) salted butter, at room temperature
1¼ cups granulated sugar
6.5 ounces white rice flour (about 1¼ cups) (such as Bob's Red Mill)
17 ounces all-purpose flour (4 cups)
2 tablespoons coarse white sparkling sugar

1 Preheat the oven to 275°F.

2 Beat the butter and granulated sugar on medium speed in a stand mixer with the paddle attachment until well blended and fluffy. Add the rice flour and beat on low speed until incorporated, scraping the bowl as needed. Gradually add the all-purpose flour; beat on low until blended, scraping the bowl occasionally.

3 Line a half-sized baking sheet with parchment paper. Press the dough into the baking sheet until very even and smooth. Bake at 275°F until the shortbread is golden in the center, 60 to 65 minutes. Reduce the oven temperature to 250°F, cover the shortbread with parchment paper, and continue to bake until a finger pressed lightly into the center of the dough leaves no imprint, 20 to 25 minutes more.

4 Set the shortbread on a cooling rack and sprinkle with the sparkling sugar. While hot, cut into 1- x 3-inch rectangles or 2-inch squares. Let cool completely on the baking sheet. After it cools, if you find that you'd like it crunchier, pop the baking sheet into a 250°F oven, covered with parchment, for about 20 minutes.

prep pointer

If you make this ahead, store the bars or squares in an airtight container at room temperature, up to 1 week, or frozen, up to 3 months.

metric equivalents

The information in the following chart is provided to help cooks outside the United States successfully use the recipes in this book. All equivalents are approximate.

cooking/oven temperatures

	Fahrenheit	Celsius	Gas Mark
Freeze Water	32° F	0° C	
Room Temp.	68° F	20° C	
Boil Water	212° F	100° C	
Bake	325° F	160° C	3
	350° F	180° C	4
	375° F	190° C	5
	400° F	200° C	6
	425° F	220° C	7
	450° F	230° C	8
Broil			Grill

liquid ingredients by volume

¼ tsp					=	1 ml		
½ tsp					=	2 ml		
1 tsp					=	5 ml		
3 tsp	=	1 Tbsp	=	½ fl oz	=	15 ml		
2 Tbsp	=	⅛ cup	=	1 fl oz	=	30 ml		
4 Tbsp	=	¼ cup	=	2 fl oz	=	60 ml		
5⅓ Tbsp	=	⅓ cup	=	3 fl oz	=	80 ml		
8 Tbsp	=	½ cup	=	4 fl oz	=	120 ml		
10⅔ Tbsp	=	⅔ cup	=	5 fl oz	=	160 ml		
12 Tbsp	=	¾ cup	=	6 fl oz	=	180 ml		
16 Tbsp	=	1 cup	=	8 fl oz	=	240 ml		
1 pt	=	2 cups	=	16 fl oz	=	480 ml		
1 qt	=	4 cups	=	32 fl oz	=	960 ml		
				33 fl oz	=	1000 ml	=	1 l

dry ingredients by weight

(To convert ounces to grams, multiply the number of ounces by 30.)

1 oz	=	¹⁄₁₆ lb	=	30 g
4 oz	=	¼ lb	=	120 g
8 oz	=	½ lb	=	240 g
12 oz	=	¾ lb	=	360 g
16 oz	=	1 lb	=	480 g

length

(To convert inches to centimeters, multiply the number of inches by 2.5.)

1 in				=	2.5 cm		
12 in	=	1 ft		=	30 cm		
36 in	=	3 ft	=	1 yd	=	90 cm	
40 in	=				100 cm	=	1 m

equivalents for different types of ingredients

Standard Cup	Fine Powder (ex. flour)	Grain (ex. rice)	Granular (ex. sugar)	Liquid Solids (ex. butter)	Liquid (ex. milk)
1	140 g	150 g	190 g	200 g	240 ml
¾	105 g	113 g	143 g	150 g	180 ml
⅔	93 g	100 g	125 g	133 g	160 ml
½	70 g	75 g	95 g	100 g	120 ml
⅓	47 g	50 g	63 g	67 g	80 ml
¼	35 g	38 g	48 g	50 g	60 ml
⅛	18 g	19 g	24 g	25 g	30 ml

index